diabetic
dinners

Quick & tasty recipes
for the entire family

24 great snacks

Kid-friendly ideas

Diabetic Dinners

Front and Back Covers

1. Tropical Trifles, page 121
2. Bows And Fresh Vegetables, page 44
3. Chili Turkey Burger, page 20
4. Spinach And Cheese Rolls, page 46
5. Roasted Pepper Sauce, page 46
6. Beef And Mandarin Salad, page 11
7. Pesto Chicken Wraps, page 74

We gratefully acknowledge the following suppliers for their generous support of our Test Kitchen and Photography Studio:

Broil King
Lagostina ®
Corelle ®
Proctor Silex ® Canada
Hamilton Beach ® Canada
Tupperware ®

Our special thanks to the following businesses for providing various props for photography:

Canhome Global
Casa Bugatti
Cherison Enterprises Inc.
Danesco Inc.
Island Pottery Inc.
Klass Works
Pfaltzgraff Canada
Pier 1 Imports
Pyrex ® Storage
Sears Canada
Stokes
The Bay
Wiltshire ®

Diabetic Dinners

First printing March 2004

National Library of Canada Cataloguing in Publication

Paré, Jean, 1927-
   Diabetic dinners / Jean Paré.

(Lifestyle series)
Includes index.
ISBN 1-896891-76-4

   1. Diabetes–Diet therapy–Recipes. 2. Entrées (Cookery) I. Title.
II. Series: Paré, Jean, 1927- . Lifestyle series.

RC662.P37 2004   641.5'6314   C2003-906078-0

Published by
Company's Coming Publishing Limited
2311 – 96 Street
Edmonton, Alberta T6N 1G3
Canada
Tel: 780 • 450-6223
Fax: 780 • 450-1857
www.companyscoming.com

Printed in Canada

COOKBOOKS

Company's Coming is a registered trademark owned by Company's Coming Publishing Limited

Visit us on-line

companyscoming.com

Who We Are   Browse Cookbooks   Cooking Tonight?   Home

everyday ingredients

feature recipes

feature recipes — Cooking tonight? Check out this month's *feature recipes*— absolutely FREE!

tips and tricks — Looking for some great kitchen helpers? *tips and tricks* is here to save the day!

reader circle — In search of answers to cooking or household questions? Do you have answers you'd like to share? Join the fun with *reader circle*, our on-line question and answer bulletin board. Our *reader circle chat room* connects you with cooks from around the world. Great for swapping recipes too!

cooking links — Other interesting and informative web-sites are just a click away with *cooking links.*

keyword search — Find cookbooks by title, description or food category using *keyword search*.

e-mail us — We want to hear from you—*e-mail us* lets you offer suggestions for upcoming titles, or share your favourite recipes.

Company's Coming
COOKBOOKS®

Canada's
most popular cookbooks!

Company's Coming

Original Series

150 Delicious Squares	Breakfasts & Brunches	Asian Cooking
Casseroles	Slow Cooker Recipes	The Cheese Book
Muffins & More	One Dish Meals	The Rookie Cook
Salads	Starters	Rush-Hour Recipes
Appetizers	Stir-Fry	Sweet Cravings
Soups & Sandwiches	Make-Ahead Meals	Year-Round Grilling
Cookies	The Potato Book	Garden Greens
Pasta	Low-Fat Cooking	Chinese Cooking
Barbecues	Low-Fat Pasta	The Pork Book
Preserves	Cook For Kids	Recipes For Leftovers
Chicken, Etc.	Stews, Chilies & Chowders	The Egg Book NEW May 1/04
Kids Cooking	Fondues	
Cooking For Two	The Beef Book	

Greatest Hits Series

Italian
Mexican

Lifestyle Series

Grilling
Diabetic Cooking
Heart-Friendly Cooking
Diabetic Dinners

Most Loved Recipe Collection

Most Loved Appetizers
Most Loved Main Courses NEW April 1/04

Special Occasion Series

Gifts from the Kitchen
Cooking for the Seasons
Home for the Holidays
Weekend Cooking
Decadent Desserts

Table of contents

The Company's Coming Story 6

Foreword 7

About Diabetes 8

The Recipes In This Cookbook 10

Main Course Dishes

      Oven, Stovetop & Barbecue 11

      Microwave 48

      Slow Cooker 60

      Two-Sided Grill 68

      Two-Way Cooking 76

Side Dishes 88

Condiments & Sauces 113

Desserts 118

Snacks 123

Measurement Tables 150

Tip Index 151

Recipe Index 151

Mail Order Form 159

The Company's Coming

Jean Paré grew up understanding that the combination of family, friends and home cooking is the essence of a good life. From her mother she learned to appreciate good cooking, while her father praised even her earliest attempts. When she left home she took with her many acquired family recipes, a love of cooking and an intriguing desire to read recipe books like novels!

"never share a recipe you wouldn't use yourself"

In 1963, when her four children had all reached school age, Jean volunteered to cater the 50th anniversary of the Vermilion School of Agriculture, now Lakeland College. Working out of her home, Jean prepared a dinner for over 1000 people which launched a flourishing catering operation that continued for over eighteen years. During that time she was provided with countless opportunities to test new ideas with immediate feedback—resulting in empty plates and contented customers! Whether preparing cocktail sandwiches for a house party or serving a hot meal for 1500 people, Jean Paré earned a reputation for good food, courteous service and reasonable prices.

"Why don't you write a cookbook?" Time and again, as requests for her recipes mounted, Jean was asked that question. Jean's response was to team up with her son, Grant Lovig, in the fall of 1980 to form Company's Coming Publishing Limited. April 14, 1981 marked the debut of "150 DELICIOUS SQUARES," the first Company's Coming cookbook in what soon would become Canada's most popular cookbook series.

Jean Paré's operation has grown steadily from the early days of working out of a spare bedroom in her home. Full-time staff includes marketing personnel located in major cities across Canada. Home Office is based in Edmonton, Alberta in a modern building constructed specially for the company.

Today the company distributes throughout Canada and the United States in addition to numerous overseas markets, all under the guidance of Jean's daughter, Gail Lovig. Best-sellers many times over in English, Company's Coming cookbooks have also been published in French and Spanish. Familiar and trusted in home kitchens around the world, Company's Coming cookbooks are offered in a variety of formats, including the original softcover series.

Jean Paré's approach to cooking has always called for quick and easy recipes using everyday ingredients. Even when travelling, she is constantly on the lookout for new ideas to share with her readers. At home, she can usually be found researching and writing recipes, or working in the company's test  kitchen. Jean continues to gain new supporters by adhering to what she calls "the golden rule of cooking:" never share a recipe you wouldn't use yourself. It's an approach that works—*millions of times over!*

foreword

Everyone with diabetes knows the importance of meal planning and eating the right foods. The delicious recipes in *Diabetic Dinners* are designed to be quick and easy to prepare, while helping to meet individual nutrition requirements.

Proper nutrition is the cornerstone for effective diabetes management. What, when and how much you eat are all critical factors in maintaining blood glucose levels. For this reason, *Diabetic Dinners* includes recipes lower in fat, sugar and sodium, as well as higher in fibre. For your assistance, detailed Nutrition Information, as well as meal-planning Choices, accompany each recipe. For more in-depth information on how we approached recipe development, read "The Recipes In This Cookbook," page 10.

Because eating timely meals is such a challenge, we've included several great snacks that fit within the parameters of most diabetics' needs. Toss several individual snack portions into your purse or into your child's backpack when on the go.

For those with a child who has diabetes, or for those who cook diabetic meals for the entire family, we've designed Kid-Friendly variations for many of the recipes. These variations cater to children's preferences and tastes. Preparing diabetic meals that are appropriate for everyone has never been easier!

A healthy lifestyle, involving plenty of physical activity and balanced meals, is so important when living with diabetes. It takes a great deal of planning to regulate these aspects of your life. That's why we've tried to simplify the task of preparing healthy meals. Our recipes call for common ingredients, saving you time, energy and money.

Make mealtime more interesting with *Diabetic Dinners*—and remember that a healthy eating plan can include your favourite foods. Enjoy the wonderful variety of fresh flavours in this collection of healthy recipes your whole family will enjoy.

Jean Paré

each recipe

has been analyzed using the most up-to-date version of the Canadian Nutrient File from Health Canada, which is based on the United States Department of Agriculture (USDA) Nutrient Data Base. If more than one ingredient is listed (such as "hard margarine or butter"), then the first ingredient is used in the analysis. Where an ingredient reads "sprinkle," "optional," or "for garnish," it is not included as part of the nutrition information.

Margaret Ng, B.Sc. (Hon), M.A.
Registered Dietitian

About Diabetes

Diabetes is a disease in which blood sugar (glucose) is not processed efficiently by the body due to the lack of insulin or insensitivity to insulin. Insulin is refined to process blood sugar into energy, otherwise it results in high glucose levels in the blood. Glucose levels are affected by digestion of carbohydrates, such as those found in grains, fruits and vegetables and milk, as well as in sugars, and by the production of glucose in the liver.

Prior to treatment, symptoms of diabetes may include increased thirst and urination, fatigue, vision changes and weight loss. Untreated, diabetes can damage the eyes, kidneys, nerves, heart and circulation system. Being physically active and maintaining a healthy body weight are keys to good living for everyone, but they are critical for those with diabetes.

In a healthy body, the pancreas produces enough insulin to enable glucose to enter cells and be used as energy. People with Type 1 diabetes have a severe lack of insulin because their pancreas produces little or none at all. In order to maintain normal blood sugar levels, many need to take insulin injections and to balance nutritional intake with activity. People with Type 2 diabetes don't produce enough insulin, or their bodies do not use it effectively. They may be able to manage the disease by weight management with diet and exercise alone, or with a combination of diet, exercise, and pills or insulin injections.

Diabetic Dinners is a cookbook filled with enticing, easy-to-prepare recipes. It follows dietary guidelines that are essentially the same for everyone—include more high-fibre, whole-grain products, and fruits and vegetables; and choose low-fat dairy products and leaner meats. People with diabetes need to consult with a registered dietitian to determine their best personal meal plan.

Most foods can be part of a diabetic meal plan. It is important to remember that some foods are more nutritious than others and therefore healthier and less damaging to our body. Alcohol, salt, fat, sugar and caffeine should be limited, but they don't necessarily need to be eliminated. Just like putting the wrong kind of gasoline in your car affects its performance, fuelling your body with poor food choices will do the same thing.

The cost of eating "premium fuel" doesn't have to be at a premium price. For example, some cuts of meat may seem pricey, but they're not when you consider that a healthy portion of steak is 4 oz. (113 g) rather than 8 oz. (225 g). Likewise, fresh fruits and vegetables fluctuate in price, so buy them in season and then compare the cost to their processed "cousin-in-a-can." Be aware of convenience foods that are often high in fat, salt and sugar. Learn to read labels carefully.

Much has been said about how carbohydrates in starchy foods and refined sugars cause blood sugars to rise. But "carbs" still need to be part of a balanced, healthy diet. Carbohydrates with fibre (generally foods which have not been highly processed, such as fruits, vegetables, beans and whole grain products) are more nutritious and better at maintaining even blood sugar levels than those from refined foods or sugars.

Advice about sugar consumption for people with diabetes has changed over the years. Small quantities of sugar distributed in foods throughout the day are now acceptable in a healthy eating plan because, in most people, blood sugar levels do not peak quickly. Up to 10% of total daily energy intake can come from sugar or added sugar in foods. For example, an 1800 calorie meal plan can include up to 180 calories from sugar, which is equivalent to 3 tbsp. (45 g) of total sugar added to foods (e.g., jam, cranberry cocktail, regular soft drinks, cakes or desserts, chocolates, etc.).

Diabetic Food Choices

Once a person has been diagnosed with diabetes, they need to meet with a registered dietitian to work out a plan outlining the types and amounts of foods for each meal and snack. Similar foods are grouped together in categories: Starch; Fruit & Vegetable; Milk; Protein (meat and meat alternatives); Fat & Oil; and Sugar. We have included these diabetic choices (exchanges) to make it easy to fit these recipes into individual meal plans. For people on insulin who require precise carbohydrate counting, the Nutrition Information provided gives the total grams of carbohydrate and dietary fibre for each recipe.

Nutrition Information

The Nutrition Information provided for each recipe in *Diabetic Dinners* tallies the calories, fat (including mono- and poly-unsaturated and saturated fats), cholesterol, carbohydrate, protein, fibre and sodium. These values include all ingredients listed in the recipe except those listed as "optional" or as a "garnish." If a range of measurements is given for an ingredient, the smaller amount is analyzed. There are Kid-Friendly Ideas given at the end of selected recipes. The Nutrition Information and Choices are provided for these if there is a significant difference from those given for the original recipe. Any other variations of the recipes are not included in the

The Recipes In This Cookbook

✦ **Artificial Sweeteners:** We did not use artificial sweeteners at the request of our Focus Group.

✦ **Cheese:** In order to lower fat content but to maintain taste, we used light, sharp (old) Cheddar cheese, part-skim mozzarella and grated, light Parmesan cheese product. We did use grated fresh Parmesan cheese, however, when flavour needed to be enhanced in selected recipes.

✦ **Fats:** We used canola or olive oil instead of margarine where possible. In some recipes, margarine or butter was better for taste, but the amount was limited. Butter should be used in moderation since it is animal fat and contains cholesterol. All fats and oils contain 9 calories per gram (compared to 4 calories per gram for carbohydrates), but vegetable or olive oil is better for your arteries when used moderately. Where possible, non-stick cookware or cooking spray was used to reduce the fats and oils used.

✦ **Meats:** In testing these recipes, we trimmed all visible fat from meats prior to cooking. We also chose leaner cuts of meat, such as boneless, skinless chicken breast halves or beef sirloin.

✦ **Milk:** We used 1% milk, unless otherwise specified, because it is a commonly acceptable low-fat milk with essentially the same nutritional values as 2% or whole milk, except fat content.

✦ **Yogurt:** We used non-fat plain or flavoured yogurt. Remember, when heated, non-fat yogurt will be runny. Use low-fat yogurt instead if heating.

✦ **Cooking Methods:** We recommend baking, grilling, steaming, poaching and stir-frying to reduce the amount of fat needed to cook an item and to retain more of the nutrients in the food. Also, drain off fat whenever possible while cooking.

If you have any questions about how these recipes, or any other food, can fit into the diet of someone with diabetes, please talk with your doctor or dietitian.

Beef And Mandarin Salad

This colourful, fresh salad is sure to get the taste buds jumping.

Lean inside round steak, trimmed of fat	12 oz.	340 g
Garlic salt	1/2 tsp.	2 mL
Can of unsweetened mandarin orange segments, drained	10 oz.	284 mL
Bag of mixed salad greens	6 oz.	170 g
Thinly sliced red onion	1/2 cup	125 mL
Thinly sliced red pepper	1/2 cup	125 mL
PARMESAN DRESSING		
Finely grated fresh Parmesan cheese	2 tbsp.	30 mL
Olive (or canola) oil	2 tbsp.	30 mL
Lemon juice	2 tbsp.	30 mL
Liquid honey	2 tsp.	10 mL
Garlic clove, minced (or 1/4 tsp., 1 mL, powder)	1	1
Salt (optional)	1/4 tsp.	1 mL
Pepper	1/4 tsp.	1 mL

Sprinkle steak with garlic salt. Preheat electric grill for 5 minutes or gas barbecue to medium-high. Cook steak on greased grill for about 5 minutes per side until desired doneness. Remove from heat. Let stand for 10 minutes. Slice into 1/4 inch (6 mm) thick strips.

Combine next 4 ingredients in large bowl. Add beef. Toss.

Parmesan Dressing: Combine all 7 ingredients in jar with tight-fitting lid. Shake well. Makes 1/3 cup (75 mL) dressing. Drizzle over salad. Toss gently. Makes 6 cups (1.5 L). Serves 4.

NUTRITION INFORMATION 1 serving: 222 Calories; 10.2 g Total Fat (6.2 g Mono, 0.8 g Poly, 2.3 g Sat); 39 mg Cholesterol; 14 g Carbohydrate; 2 g Fibre; 20 g Protein; 247 mg Sodium

CHOICES 1 Fruit & Vegetable; 3 Protein

Pictured on front cover.

Apple Curry Wraps

The unique combination of mild curry with a sweet apple tang will tantalize your taste buds. Use different flavours of tortillas for variety in colour and flavour.

Olive (or canola) oil	2 tsp.	10 mL
Sirloin steak, cut across grain into 1/8 inch (3 mm) thick slices	1/2 lb.	225 g
Chopped onion	1/4 cup	60 mL
Garlic cloves, minced (or 1/2 tsp., 2 mL, powder)	2	2
Mild green curry paste	1 1/2 tsp.	7 mL
Apple juice	1/3 cup	75 mL
Frozen peas, thawed	3/4 cup	175 mL
Medium cooking apple (such as McIntosh), peeled, cored and diced	1	1
Non-fat plain yogurt	1/2 cup	125 mL
Hot, cooked, short grain brown rice (about 1/2 cup, 125 mL, uncooked)	1 1/3 cups	325 mL
Large flour tortillas (10 inch, 25 cm, diameter), warmed (see Tip, page 15)	4	4

Heat wok or large non-stick frying pan on medium until very hot. Add olive oil. Add beef, onion and garlic. Stir-fry for about 3 minutes, until beef is no longer pink inside and onion is softened.

Add curry paste and apple juice. Heat and stir until boiling.

Add peas and apple. Stir. Simmer, uncovered, for about 1 minute until heated through. Remove from heat.

Add yogurt. Stir.

Divide and spoon rice down centre of each tortilla. Divide and spoon beef mixture over rice. Fold sides and 1 end of tortilla over filling. Roll up from bottom to enclose filling. Makes 4 wraps.

NUTRITION INFORMATION 1 wrap: 439 Calories; 11.2 g Total Fat (5.3 g Mono, 2 g Poly, 2.7 g Sat); 41 mg Cholesterol; 58 g Carbohydrate; 5 g Fibre; 26 g Protein; 295 mg Sodium

CHOICES 3 Starch; 1 Fruit & Vegetable; 2 1/2 Protein; 1/2 Fat & Oil

(continued on next page)

Kid-Friendly Idea

Omit curry paste. Substitute same amount of cooked long grain white rice for the brown.

NUTRITION INFORMATION 1 wrap: 431 Calories; 10 g Total Fat (4.8 g Mono, 1.7 g Poly, 2.6 g Sat); 41 mg Cholesterol; 58 g Carbohydrate; 4 g Fibre; 26 g Protein; 295 mg Sodium

CHOICES: 3 Starch; 1 Fruit & Vegetable; 2 1/2 Protein; 1/2 Fat & Oil

Mushroom Beef Burgers

A hearty and tasty make-ahead meal everyone will love.

Canola oil	**1 tbsp.**	**15 mL**
Thinly sliced onion	**1 cup**	**250 mL**
Sliced fresh white mushrooms	**2 cups**	**500 mL**
Seasoned salt	**1/4 tsp.**	**1 mL**
Extra lean ground beef	**1 lb.**	**454 g**
Finely chopped onion	**1/2 cup**	**125 mL**
Finely chopped fresh parsley (or 2 1/4 tsp., 11 mL, flakes)	**3 tbsp.**	**50 mL**
Barbecue sauce	**2 tbsp.**	**30 mL**
Pepper	**1/4 tsp.**	**1 mL**
Salsa	**1/2 cup**	**125 mL**
Hamburger buns, split and lightly toasted	**4**	**4**
Large tomato, sliced	**1**	**1**
Thinly sliced English cucumber (with peel)	**1/2 cup**	**125 mL**

Heat canola oil in large non-stick frying pan on medium. Add onion. Cook for 5 to 10 minutes, stirring occasionally, until onion is softened. Increase heat to medium-high.

Add mushrooms and seasoned salt. Cook for about 5 minutes, stirring occasionally, until mushrooms begin to brown.

Combine next 5 ingredients in large bowl. Press into 4 patties. Preheat electric grill for 5 minutes or gas barbecue to medium. Cook on greased grill for about 5 minutes per side until no longer pink inside. Spread salsa on both sides of each bun. Divide and layer patty, mushroom mixture, tomato and cucumber on bottom half of each bun. Cover with top halves. Makes 4 burgers.

NUTRITION INFORMATION 1 burger: 382 Calories; 15.7 g Total Fat (7.3 g Mono, 2 g Poly, 4.5 g Sat); 59 mg Cholesterol; 34 g Carbohydrate; 4 g Fibre; 27 g Protein; 528 mg Sodium

CHOICES 2 Starch; 3 Protein; 1 1/2 Fat & Oil

Beef And Asparagus

Fresh, tender-crisp vegetables and beef are so good in an Asian-influenced sauce. Sprinkles of sesame seeds dress up this colourful dish. Serve with steamed broccoli and brown or white rice.

Dry sherry	1 tbsp.	15 mL
Low-sodium soy sauce	1 tbsp.	15 mL
Sesame (or canola) oil	1 tsp.	5 mL
Garlic cloves, minced (or 1/2 tsp., 2 mL, powder)	2	2
Finely grated, peeled gingerroot	1/2 tsp.	2 mL
Sirloin steak, cut across grain into 1/8 inch (3 mm) thick slices	1 lb.	454 g
Low-sodium prepared beef broth	1/3 cup	75 mL
Cornstarch	2 tsp.	10 mL
Low-sodium soy sauce	2 tbsp.	30 mL
Sweet (or regular) chili sauce	1 tbsp.	15 mL
Canola oil	2 tsp.	10 mL
Canola oil	2 tsp.	10 mL
Fresh asparagus, trimmed of tough ends and cut into 2 inch (5 cm) lengths	12 oz.	340 g
Small cauliflower florets (4 oz., 113 g)	1 cup	250 mL
Small onion, cut lengthwise into 6 wedges	1	1
Slivered red pepper (2 1/2 oz., 70 g)	1/2 cup	125 mL
Sesame seeds, toasted (see Tip, page 63), optional	1 tsp.	5 mL

Combine first 5 ingredients in medium bowl.

Cut beef slices into 2 inch (5 cm) strips. Add to sherry mixture. Stir until coated. Cover. Marinate at room temperature for 15 minutes.

Stir broth into cornstarch in small cup until smooth. Add second amount of soy sauce and chili sauce. Stir. Set aside.

Heat wok or large non-stick frying pan on medium-high until very hot. Add first amount of canola oil. Add beef mixture. Stir-fry for 2 minutes. Transfer to plate.

Add second amount of canola oil to same wok. Add next 4 ingredients. Stir-fry for 3 to 4 minutes until asparagus is bright green and tender-crisp. Add beef mixture. Stir cornstarch mixture. Add to beef mixture. Cook for about 1 minute, stirring constantly, until boiling and thickened.

Sprinkle with sesame seeds. Makes 4 cups (1 L). Serves 4.

(continued on next page)

NUTRITION INFORMATION 1 serving: 292 Calories; 16.1 g Total Fat (7.5 g Mono, 2.4 g Poly, 4.6 g Sat); 56 mg Cholesterol; 11 g Carbohydrate; 3 g Fibre; 25 g Protein; 554 mg Sodium

CHOICES 1 Fruit & Vegetable; 3 1/2 Protein; 1 Fat & Oil

Pictured on page 17.

Kid-Friendly Idea

Substitute ketchup for the chili sauce. Substitute same amount of your child's favourite vegetables for the asparagus, cauliflower, onion and/or red pepper.

NUTRITION INFORMATION 1 serving: 307 Calories; 16.1 g Total Fat (7.5 g Mono, 2.4 g Poly, 4.6 g Sat); 56 mg Cholesterol;15 g Carbohydrate; 3 g Fibre; 25 g Protein; 574 mg Sodium

CHOICES 1 Fruit & Vegetable; 3 1/2 Protein; 1 Fat & Oil

To warm tortillas, wrap in foil or damp tea towel and heat in 200ºF (95ºC) oven for 10 minutes. Or sprinkle individual tortillas with water. Microwave, 1 or 2 at a time, on high (100%) for 20 seconds.

Lemon Garlic Steaks

A good recipe to make ahead. So simple, yet so delicious. The lemon juice adds a fresh zing to the marinade. Serve with a fresh garden salad and cooked mushrooms.

Chopped fresh parsley (not dried)	**1/4 cup**	**60 mL**
Lemon juice	**3 tbsp.**	**50 mL**
Sweet (or regular) chili sauce	**2 tbsp.**	**30 mL**
Olive (or canola) oil	**1 tbsp.**	**15 mL**
Garlic cloves, minced (or 1/2 tsp., 2 mL, powder)	**2**	**2**
Pepper	**1 tsp.**	**5 mL**
New York cut steak, trimmed of fat and cut in half	**1 lb.**	**454 g**

Combine first 6 ingredients in medium bowl.

Add steak. Turn until coated. Cover. Marinate for at least 8 hours or overnight. Drain and discard marinade. Preheat electric grill for 5 minutes or gas barbecue to medium-high. Cook steak on greased grill for about 5 minutes per side until desired doneness. Serves 4.

NUTRITION INFORMATION 1 serving: 203 Calories; 12.1 g Total Fat (5.6 g Mono, 0.5 g Poly, 4.4 g Sat); 46 mg Cholesterol; 2 g Carbohydrate; trace Fibre; 20 g Protein; 98 mg Sodium

CHOICES 3 Protein; 1/2 Fat & Oil

Pictured on page 89.

Kid-Friendly Idea

Omit the garlic and use only 1/4 tsp. (1 mL) pepper.

1. Fried Rice, page 98
2. Oriental Citrus Chicken, page 21
3. Beef And Asparagus, page 14

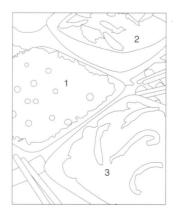

Pineapple Chicken Balls

Chicken, pineapple and green pepper in a sweet and sour sauce that's perfect over hot rice.

Large egg	1	1
Sliced green onion	1/4 cup	60 mL
Quick-cooking rolled oats (not instant)	1/2 cup	125 mL
Low-sodium chicken bouillon powder	1 tsp.	5 mL
Dried thyme	1/4 tsp.	1 mL
Lean ground chicken (or turkey)	1 lb.	454 g
Can of pineapple tidbits (with juice)	14 oz.	398 mL
White vinegar	3 tbsp.	50 mL
Brown sugar, packed	2 tbsp.	30 mL
Low-sodium soy sauce	2 tbsp.	30 mL
Green medium pepper, diced	1	1
Water	3 tbsp.	50 mL
Cornstarch	1 1/2 tbsp.	25 mL

Combine first 5 ingredients in medium bowl.

Add chicken. Mix well. Shape into about forty 1 inch (2.5 cm) balls. Arrange in single layer on greased baking sheet with sides. Bake, uncovered, in 400°F (205°C) oven for about 15 minutes until browned and no longer pink inside.

Combine next 5 ingredients in large frying pan. Heat on medium-high, stirring occasionally, until boiling. Reduce heat to medium-low. Cover. Simmer for 3 minutes.

Stir water into cornstarch in small dish until smooth. Stir into sauce until boiling and thickened. Add meatballs. Stir. Heat, stirring occasionally, for 5 minutes. Serves 4.

NUTRITION INFORMATION 1 serving: 325 Calories; 5.9 g Total Fat (1.8 g Mono, 1.4 g Poly, 1.5 g Sat); 133 mg Cholesterol; 39 g Carbohydrate; 3 g Fibre; 29 g Protein; 436 mg Sodium

CHOICES 1 Starch; 2 Fruit & Vegetable; 3 Protein

1. Zucchini Pepper Combo, page 105
2. Poached Spice Chicken, page 22

Chili Turkey Burgers

Hearty burgers that are great broiled or grilled. They have a tender texture and a spicy bite.

Lean ground turkey	3/4 lb.	340 g
Egg whites (large)	2	2
Medium jalapeño pepper, seeds and ribs removed (see Tip, page 113), finely diced	1	1
Green onions, finely chopped	2	2
Garlic cloves, minced (or 1/2 tsp., 2 mL, powder)	2	2
Chili powder	1 tsp.	5 mL
Paprika	1 tsp.	5 mL
Garlic and herb no-salt seasoning (such as Mrs. Dash)	2 tsp.	10 mL
Pepper	1/4 tsp.	1 mL
Slices of light Monterey Jack cheese, (about 2 oz., 57 g, total), optional	4	4
Whole wheat hamburger buns (or Kaiser rolls), split and toasted	4	4
Fat-free salad dressing (or mayonnaise), optional	1/4 cup	60 mL
Prepared mustard	2 tbsp.	30 mL
Salsa (optional)	1/4 cup	60 mL
Red onion slices	4	4
Lettuce leaves	4	4
Large tomato slices	4	4

Put first 9 ingredients into medium bowl. Mix well. Divide and shape into 4 patties about 4 inches (10 cm) in diameter. Broil on centre rack in oven for 4 to 5 minutes per side until juices run clear and patties are no longer pink inside.

Place cheese slices on patties to melt.

Spread bottom half of each bun with salad dressing, mustard and salsa. Place 1 patty on each bottom half. Top with onion, lettuce and tomato. Cover with top halves. Makes 4 burgers.

NUTRITION INFORMATION 1 burger: 297 Calories; 11.4 g Total Fat (4.6 g Mono, 2.7 g Poly, 2.8 g Sat); 63 mg Cholesterol; 25 g Carbohydrate; 3 g Fibre; 24 g Protein; 403 mg Sodium

CHOICES 1 1/2 Starch; 3 Protein; 1/2 Fat & Oil

Pictured on front cover.

Oriental Citrus Chicken

Tender chicken and snap peas are so good in this orange sauce. Perfect served over rice.

Orange juice	3/4 cup	175 mL
Cornstarch	1 tbsp.	15 mL
Hoisin sauce	2 tbsp.	30 mL
Oyster sauce	1 tbsp.	15 mL
Rice vinegar (or lemon juice)	1 tbsp.	15 mL
Brown sugar, packed	2 tsp.	10 mL
Finely grated orange zest	1 tsp.	5 mL
Olive (or canola) oil	2 tsp.	10 mL
Boneless, skinless chicken breast halves, cut into thin strips	3/4 lb.	340 g
Garlic powder (optional)	1/2 tsp.	2 mL
Ground ginger	1/2 tsp.	2 mL
Chopped onion	1 cup	250 mL
Chopped celery	1 cup	250 mL
Chopped carrot	2/3 cup	150 mL
Low-sodium prepared chicken broth	1/2 cup	125 mL
Package of sugar snap peas (about 2 cups, 500 mL), trimmed	8 oz.	227 g
Sesame seeds, toasted (see Tip, page 63), optional	2 tsp.	10 mL

Stir orange juice into cornstarch in small bowl until smooth. Add next 5 ingredients. Stir. Set aside.

Heat wok or large non-stick frying pan on medium-high. Add olive oil. Add chicken. Sprinkle with garlic and ginger. Stir-fry for about 4 minutes until chicken is no longer pink inside.

Add onion, celery and carrot. Stir-fry for 2 minutes.

Add broth and peas. Stir. Reduce heat to medium. Cover. Simmer for 3 to 5 minutes until carrot is tender-crisp and peas are bright green. Stir cornstarch mixture. Add to chicken mixture. Heat and stir until mixture is boiling and thickened.

Sprinkle with sesame seeds. Makes 6 cups (1.5 L). Serves 4.

NUTRITION INFORMATION 1 serving: 270 Calories; 5.3 g Total Fat (2.5 g Mono, 1.1 g Poly, 1 g Sat); 61 mg Cholesterol; 28 g Carbohydrate; 3 g Fibre; 27 g Protein; 641 mg Sodium

CHOICES 2 Fruit & Vegetable; 3 1/2 Protein; 1/2 Sugar

Pictured on page 17.

Poached Spice Chicken

Lovely, moist chicken with a sweet and spicy sauce. Serve with Roasted Cauliflower, page 102, or Oven-Fried Vegetables, page 112.

SWEET AND SPICY SAUCE		
Low-sodium prepared chicken broth	1 1/2 cups	375 mL
Orange juice	1 cup	250 mL
Dry white wine (or low-sodium prepared chicken broth)	1/2 cup	125 mL
Liquid honey	2 tbsp.	30 mL
Whole green cardamom, bruised (see Tip, page 23)	6	6
Cinnamon stick (4 inch, 10 cm, length)	1	1
Ground cumin	1/2 tsp.	2 mL
Ground coriander	1/2 tsp.	2 mL
Chili powder	1/4 tsp.	1 mL
Boneless, skinless chicken breast halves (4 – 6 oz., 113 – 170 g, each)	4	4
HERB COUSCOUS		
Low-sodium prepared chicken broth	3/4 cup	175 mL
Couscous	3/4 cup	175 mL
Olive (or canola) oil	1 tsp.	5 mL
Chopped fresh mint leaves (or 1 1/2 tsp., 7 mL, dried)	2 tbsp.	30 mL
Chopped fresh cilantro (or fresh parsley), optional	2 tbsp.	30 mL

Sweet And Spicy Sauce: Combine first 9 ingredients in medium frying pan. Heat and stir on medium until boiling. Reduce heat to medium-low.

Add chicken. Cook, uncovered, for about 15 minutes, turning once, until chicken is no longer pink inside. Remove chicken to 2 quart (2 L) casserole. Cover to keep warm. Boil remaining sauce on medium-high for about 15 minutes until reduced by half. Strain into small bowl, discarding solids. Makes about 1 1/3 cups (325 mL) sauce. Pour over chicken. Cover to keep warm.

Herb Couscous: Bring broth to a boil in medium saucepan. Remove from heat.

Immediately add couscous and olive oil. Stir. Cover. Let stand for 5 minutes. Fluff with fork.

Add mint and cilantro. Stir. Makes 2 1/4 cups (550 mL) couscous. Serve with chicken and sauce. Serves 4.

(continued on next page)

NUTRITION INFORMATION 1 serving: 368 Calories; 3.5 g Total Fat (1.4 g Mono, 0.6 g Poly, 0.7 g Sat); 66 mg Cholesterol; 45 g Carbohydrate; 2 g Fibre; 32 g Protein; 368 mg Sodium

CHOICES 2 Starch; 1/2 Fruit & Vegetable; 4 Protein; 1 Sugar

Pictured on page 18.

Kid-Friendly Idea

The spices are somewhat exotic, so children may not readily enjoy the flavour. Reduce spices the first time around to let kids gradually become familiar with the taste.

To bruise cardamom, pound cardamom pods with a mallet or press with the flat side of a wide knife to "bruise" or crack them. Open slightly.

Chicken Mushroom Rolls

Thick, creamy cheese sauce covers pasta rolls flavoured with rosemary and thyme.

Whole wheat lasagna noodles	**10**	**10**
Boiling water	**12 cups**	**3 L**
Salt	**1 tbsp.**	**15 mL**
CHICKEN MUSHROOM FILLING		
Olive (or canola) oil	**1 tsp.**	**5 mL**
Lean ground chicken	**1 lb.**	**454 g**
Finely chopped onion	**1/4 cup**	**60 mL**
Garlic (or regular) chili sauce	**1 tsp.**	**5 mL**
Finely chopped fresh white mushrooms	**1 1/2 cups**	**375 mL**
Finely chopped red pepper	**1/3 cup**	**75 mL**
Garlic and herb no-salt seasoning (such as Mrs. Dash)	**1 tsp.**	**5 mL**
Pepper	**1/4 tsp.**	**1 mL**
All-purpose flour	**2 tbsp.**	**30 mL**
Low-sodium prepared chicken broth	**2/3 cup**	**150 mL**
Finely chopped fresh thyme (or 1/4 tsp., 1 mL, dried)	**1 tsp.**	**5 mL**
Finely chopped fresh rosemary (or 1/4 tsp., 1 mL, dried)	**1 tsp.**	**5 mL**
PARMESAN CHEESE SAUCE		
Skim milk	**2 cups**	**500 mL**
All-purpose flour	**2 tbsp.**	**30 mL**
Finely grated fresh Parmesan cheese	**1/4 cup**	**60 mL**
Salt	**1/4 tsp.**	**1 mL**
Ground nutmeg, sprinkle		

Cook noodles in boiling water and salt in large uncovered pot or Dutch oven for 10 to 12 minutes, stirring occasionally, until tender but firm. Drain. Rinse. Drain well.

Chicken Mushroom Filling: Heat olive oil in large non-stick frying pan on medium. Add chicken, onion and chili sauce. Scramble-fry for about 7 minutes until onion is softened and chicken is no longer pink.

Add next 4 ingredients. Cook, stirring often, until most liquid is evaporated.

Sprinkle with flour. Stir. Add broth, thyme and rosemary. Heat and stir until boiling and thickened. Transfer to medium bowl. Let stand for about 15 minutes until cool. Makes 2 1/2 cups (625 mL) filling. Spread 1/4 cup (60 mL) filling down length of each noodle. Roll up, jelly roll-style. Place rolls, seam-side down, in greased 9 x 13 inch (22 x 33 cm) pan.

(continued on next page)

Parmesan Cheese Sauce: Stir milk into flour in small saucepan until smooth. Heat and stir on medium for about 8 minutes until boiling and thickened.

Add cheese, salt and nutmeg. Stir. Pour over noodle rolls. Spread sauce evenly. Cover with greased foil. Bake in 350°F (175°C) oven for 30 minutes. Remove foil. Broil, uncovered, for about 10 minutes until bubbling and golden. Makes 10 rolls. Serves 4 to 6.

NUTRITION INFORMATION 1 serving: 445 Calories; 7.9 g Total Fat (2.6 g Mono, 1.4 g Poly, 2.6 g Sat); 87 mg Cholesterol; 54 g Carbohydrate; 5 g Fibre; 41 g Protein; 558 mg Sodium

CHOICES 2 1/2 Starch; 1/2 Fruit & Vegetable; 1 Milk; 4 1/2 Protein

Kid-Friendly Idea

Substitute same amount of regular lasagna noodles for the whole wheat. Omit mushrooms and red pepper. Use 2 cups (500 mL) frozen mixed vegetables (thawed). Omit fresh herbs.

NUTRITION INFORMATION 1 roll: 203 Calories; 3.3 g Total Fat (1.1 g Mono, 0.6 g Poly, 1.1 g Sat); 35 mg Cholesterol; 26 g Carbohydrate; 2 g Fibre; 17 g Protein; 241 mg Sodium

CHOICES 1 Starch; 1/2 Fruit & Vegetable; 1/2 Milk; 1 1/2 Protein

To make uniform-sized meatballs, use a small scoop (looks like a miniature ice cream scoop and is available in various sizes at kitchen stores and at hotel and restaurant supply stores). Or press beef mixture into a square or rectangle shape, same thickness all over. Cut into smaller squares of equal size. Roll each square into a ball.

Chicken And Pea Risotto

Parmesan cheese and mint enhance the flavour of this creamy risotto. Peas add crunchiness.

Low-sodium prepared chicken broth	**7 cups**	**1.75 L**
Boneless, skinless chicken breast halves	**1 lb.**	**454 g**
Olive (or canola) oil	**2 tsp.**	**10 mL**
Finely chopped onion	**1 cup**	**250 mL**
Garlic cloves, minced (or 1/2 tsp., 2 mL, powder)	**2**	**2**
Lemon pepper	**1/2 tsp.**	**2 mL**
Uncooked arborio rice	**1 cup**	**250 mL**
Uncooked long grain brown rice	**1 cup**	**250 mL**
Dry white wine (or low-sodium prepared chicken broth)	**1/2 cup**	**125 mL**
Frozen peas	**1 cup**	**250 mL**
Chopped fresh basil (or 1 1/2 tsp., 7 mL, dried)	**2 tbsp.**	**30 mL**
Chopped fresh mint leaves (or 3/4 tsp., 4 mL, dried)	**1 tbsp.**	**15 mL**
Finely grated fresh Parmesan cheese	**1/3 cup**	**75 mL**

Bring broth to a boil in medium saucepan. Cover. Reduce to lowest heat.

Sear chicken in olive oil in large saucepan on medium-high until well browned on each side. Remove chicken, reserving drippings and brown bits in saucepan. Cut chicken into 1/2 inch (12 mm) pieces. Cover to keep warm.

Add onion, garlic and lemon pepper to drippings. Heat and stir on medium for about 5 minutes, scraping up any brown bits from bottom of saucepan, until onion is softened.

Add arborio rice and brown rice. Stir well.

Add wine. Heat and stir until wine is absorbed. Add warm broth, 1 cup (250 mL) at a time, stirring constantly, until broth is absorbed. This will take about 30 minutes.

Add chicken, peas, basil and mint. Heat and stir until heated through.

Remove from heat. Stir in Parmesan cheese until melted. Makes 9 cups (2.25 L). Serves 6.

NUTRITION INFORMATION 1 serving: 436 Calories; 6 g Total Fat (2.4 g Mono, 0.9 g Poly, 1.9 g Sat); 49 mg Cholesterol; 61 g Carbohydrate; 3 g Fibre; 30 g Protein; 886 mg Sodium

CHOICES 3 1/2 Starch; 1/2 Fruit & Vegetable; 3 Protein

Blackened Snapper

The delicious spices on this tender fish are cooled down with a minty yogurt sauce. You may want to cook this on the barbecue to avoid the household smoke detector from sounding.

All-purpose flour	2 tbsp.	30 mL
Parsley flakes	1 tbsp.	15 mL
Finely grated lemon zest	2 tsp.	10 mL
Paprika	2 tsp.	10 mL
Pepper	1 tsp.	5 mL
Garlic powder	3/4 tsp.	4 mL
Onion powder	3/4 tsp.	4 mL
Cayenne pepper	1/4 tsp.	1 mL
Snapper fillets, skinned	1 lb.	454 g
Canola oil	2 tbsp.	30 mL
COOL YOGURT SAUCE		
Non-fat plain yogurt	2/3 cup	150 mL
Chopped fresh mint leaves	1 tbsp.	15 mL

Combine first 8 ingredients in small dish.

Lay fillets on large sheet of waxed paper. Divide and sprinkle flour mixture on both sides of fillets. Press fillets into any loose mixture left on paper.

Heat large non-stick frying pan on medium-high until hot. Add 1 tbsp. (15 mL) canola oil. Tilt pan to coat. Add 1/2 of fillets. Cook for about 1 1/2 minutes per side until browned and fish flakes easily when tested with fork. Some smoking will occur. Transfer fish to plate. Keep warm. Repeat with remaining canola oil and fillets.

Cool Yogurt Sauce: Combine yogurt and mint in small bowl. Makes 2/3 cup (150 mL) sauce. Serve with fish. Serves 4.

NUTRITION INFORMATION 1 serving: 221 Calories; 8.7 g Total Fat (4.4 g Mono, 2.7 g Poly, 0.9 g Sat); 43 mg Cholesterol; 8 g Carbohydrate; 1 g Fibre; 26 g Protein; 106 mg Sodium

CHOICES 1 Milk; 3 Protein

Kid-Friendly Idea

Omit cayenne pepper and reduce or omit pepper. Omit mint in the sauce.

Shrimp And Asparagus Stir-Fry

Bright green asparagus lends crunch and flavour to this light, summery stir-fry. Serve this quick, easy-to-prepare dish with a bowl of steaming jasmine (or other) rice.

Low-sodium prepared chicken broth	1/4 cup	60 mL
Cornstarch	1 tsp.	5 mL
Low-sodium soy sauce	1 1/2 tbsp.	25 mL
Chili paste (sambal oelek)	1/2 tsp.	2 mL
Canola oil	2 tsp.	10 mL
Sliced green onion	1/3 cup	75 mL
Garlic cloves, minced (or 1/2 tsp., 2 mL, powder)	2	2
Finely grated, peeled gingerroot	1 – 2 tsp.	5 – 10 mL
Raw medium shrimp, peeled and deveined	1 lb.	454 g
Fresh asparagus, trimmed of tough ends, cut into 1 inch (2.5 cm) pieces	1 lb.	454 g
Sesame seeds, toasted (see Tip, page 63), optional	1 tbsp.	15 mL

Stir broth into cornstarch in small dish until smooth. Add soy sauce and chili paste. Stir. Set aside.

Heat wok or large non-stick frying pan on medium-high until very hot. Add canola oil. Add green onion, garlic and ginger. Stir-fry for 1 to 2 minutes until fragrant.

Add shrimp and asparagus. Stir cornstarch mixture. Add to shrimp mixture. Stir-fry for about 5 minutes until shrimp are pink and curled, asparagus is tender-crisp and sauce is thickened.

Sprinkle with sesame seeds. Makes 4 1/2 cups (1.1 L). Serves 4.

NUTRITION INFORMATION 1 serving: 176 Calories; 4.5 g Total Fat (1.7 g Mono, 1.5 g Poly, 0.6 g Sat); 173 mg Cholesterol; 8 g Carbohydrate; 2 g Fibre; 26 g Protein; 397 mg Sodium

CHOICES 1/2 Fruit & Vegetable; 3 1/2 Protein

Pictured on page 35.

Creamy Fish Stew

Tender pieces of fish and baby clams taste delicious in this creamy stew. Asparagus and green beans add a splash of colour and a pleasing texture.

Hard margarine (or butter)	2 tsp.	10 mL
Finely chopped onion	1/2 cup	125 mL
All-purpose flour	2 tbsp.	30 mL
Dry white wine (or low-sodium prepared chicken broth)	1/2 cup	125 mL
Milk	1 cup	250 mL
Low-sodium prepared chicken broth	1 cup	250 mL
Fish fillets (such as cod or halibut), skinned and cut into 2 inch (5 cm) pieces	1 lb.	454 g
Fresh (or frozen, thawed) cut green beans	1 cup	250 mL
Fresh asparagus, trimmed of tough ends and cut into 1 inch (2.5 cm) pieces	1/2 lb.	225 g
Cans of whole baby clams (5 oz., 142 g, each), rinsed and drained	2	2
Chopped fresh dill (or 3/4 – 2 1/4 tsp., 4 – 11 mL, dill weed)	1 – 3 tbsp.	15 – 50 mL

Melt margarine in large pot or Dutch oven on medium. Add onion. Cook for 5 to 10 minutes, stirring often, until onion is softened.

Add flour. Heat and stir for 1 minute. Add wine, milk and broth. Heat and stir for about 5 minutes until boiling and thickened.

Add fish, green beans and asparagus. Bring to a boil. Cover. Reduce heat to medium-low. Simmer for about 10 minutes, without stirring, until fish flakes easily when tested with fork and vegetables are tender-crisp.

Add clams and dill. Stir until heated through. Makes 6 3/4 cups (1.7 L). Serves 4.

NUTRITION INFORMATION 1 serving: 270 Calories; 4.5 g Total Fat (1.7 g Mono, 0.8 g Poly, 1.1 g Sat); 80 mg Cholesterol; 15 g Carbohydrate; 2 g Fibre; 36 g Protein; 328 mg Sodium

CHOICES 1 Fruit & Vegetable; 1/2 Milk; 5 Protein

Parmesan Crumbed Fish

Snapper and sole work well in this recipe, but so will your favourite kind of fish.

Large egg	1	1
Milk	2 tsp.	10 mL
Fine dry bread crumbs (1/2 oz., 14 g)	3/4 cup	175 mL
Finely grated fresh Parmesan cheese	3 tbsp.	50 mL
Chopped fresh parsley (or 2 1/4 tsp., 11 mL, flakes)	3 tbsp.	50 mL
Salt, sprinkle		
All-purpose flour	3 tbsp.	50 mL
Fish fillets (such as snapper), skinned	1 1/2 lbs.	680 g
Canola oil	1 1/2 tbsp.	25 mL

Beat egg and milk with fork in shallow dish.

Combine next 4 ingredients in separate shallow dish.

Measure flour onto sheet of waxed paper. Cut fish into 6 portions. Dredge fish in flour. Dip into egg mixture. Press into crumb mixture until coated.

Heat canola oil in large non-stick frying pan on medium. Add fish. Cook for about 3 minutes per side until fish is golden and flakes easily when tested with fork. Serves 6.

NUTRITION INFORMATION   1 serving: 223 Calories; 7.3 g Total Fat (3.2 g Mono, 1.8 g Poly, 1.6 g Sat); 73 mg Cholesterol; 14 g Carbohydrate; 1 g Fibre; 24 g Protein; 255 mg Sodium

CHOICES   1 Starch; 1/2 Fruit & Vegetable; 3 Protein

Pictured on page 35.

To Make Ahead: Crumb fish. Cover. Chill for up to 4 hours.

Marinated Halibut Skewers

Flaky chunks of halibut with a generous sprinkling of dill. Great on the barbecue, too! Serve with Tropical Yogurt Topping, page 116, for a summertime feel.

Lime juice	2 tbsp.	30 mL
Dry white wine (or apple juice)	2 tbsp.	30 mL
Chopped fresh dill (or 3/4 tsp., 4 mL, dill weed)	1 tbsp.	15 mL
Garlic cloves, minced (or 1/4 – 1/2 tsp., 1 – 2 mL, powder), optional	1 – 2	1 – 2
Minced peeled gingerroot	1 tsp.	5 mL
Sesame oil (optional)	2 tsp.	10 mL
Fresh (or frozen, thawed) halibut steaks, skin removed, boned and cut into 1 1/4 inch (3 cm) cubes	1 1/4 lbs.	560 g
Bamboo skewers (6 inch, 15 cm, length), soaked in water for 10 minutes	8	8

Combine first 6 ingredients in medium bowl.

Add fish. Stir until coated. Cover. Marinate in refrigerator for 1 hour. Stir. Remove fish. Discard marinade.

Thread 3 fish cubes, crosswise through grain of fish, close together onto each skewer. Place on greased wire rack set in broiler pan. Broil on top rack in oven for about 8 minutes, turning carefully at halftime, until fish flakes easily when carefully tested with fork. Makes 8 skewers. Serves 4.

NUTRITION INFORMATION 1 serving: 162 Calories; 3.2 g Total Fat (1.1 g Mono, 1.2 g Poly, 0.5 g Sat); 45 mg Cholesterol; 1 g Carbohydrate; trace Fibre; 29 g Protein; 76 mg Sodium

CHOICES 4 Protein

Kid-Friendly Ideas

Use apple juice instead of white wine. You might also choose to omit ginger.

Preheat gas barbecue to medium. Place skewers on well-greased grill. Close lid. Cook for 6 to 8 minutes, turning carefully at halftime, until fish flakes easily when carefully tested with fork.

Fish Parcels

Tender fish topped with tomato and fresh dill. The warm aroma will excite your senses.

Fish fillets (such as red snapper), skinned	**1 1/4 lbs.**	**560 g**
Finely chopped tomato	**1 cup**	**250 mL**
Lemon juice	**3 tbsp.**	**50 mL**
Chopped fresh dill (or 3/4 tsp., 4 mL, dill weed)	**1 tbsp.**	**15 mL**
Olive (or canola) oil	**1 tbsp.**	**15 mL**
Garlic salt	**1/2 tsp.**	**2 mL**
Pepper	**1/4 tsp.**	**1 mL**

Cut fish into 4 portions. Place each portion on greased 10 x 12 inch (25 x 30 cm) sheet of foil.

Combine remaining 6 ingredients in small bowl. Divide and spoon over each portion of fish. Bring long sides of foil together. Fold over to form parcel. Fold short sides in to secure. Place parcels on ungreased baking sheet. Bake in 400°F (205ºC) oven for 15 minutes. Carefully open parcel. Fish should flake easily when tested with fork. Serves 4.

NUTRITION INFORMATION 1 serving: 182 Calories; 5.4 g Total Fat (2.9 g Mono, 1 g Poly, 0.9 g Sat); 52 mg Cholesterol; 3 g Carbohydrate; trace Fibre; 29 g Protein; 241 mg Sodium

CHOICES 4 Protein

Pictured on page 35.

Pork And Pineapple Stir-Fry

Spicy, tangy and sweet—pork and pineapple are a great combination. Serve with jasmine rice. This is excellent.

Low-sodium prepared chicken broth	1/4 cup	60 mL
Cornstarch	2 tsp.	10 mL
Hoisin sauce	2 tbsp.	30 mL
Low-sodium soy sauce	2 tbsp.	30 mL
Canola oil	1 tsp.	5 mL
Pork tenderloin, trimmed of fat and thinly sliced	3/4 lb.	340 g
Canola oil	1 tsp.	5 mL
Small red onion, cut into thin wedges	1	1
Garlic clove, minced (or 1/4 tsp., 1 mL, powder)	1	1
Finely grated, peeled gingerroot (or 1/4 tsp., 1 mL, ground ginger)	1 tsp.	5 mL
Chili paste (sambal oelek)	1 tsp.	5 mL
Fresh snow peas	1 cup	250 mL
Can of pineapple slices, drained and cut into 3/4 inch (2 cm) pieces	14 oz.	398 mL
Whole cashews, toasted (see Tip, page 63), optional	1/4 cup	60 mL

Stir broth into cornstarch in small cup until smooth. Add hoisin sauce and soy sauce. Stir. Set aside.

Heat wok or large frying pan on medium-high until very hot. Add first amount of canola oil. Add pork. Stir-fry until pork is browned. Transfer to bowl.

Heat second amount of canola oil in same wok on medium-high. Add next 4 ingredients. Stir-fry for 1 to 2 minutes until fragrant.

Add peas and pineapple. Stir. Add pork. Stir.

Stir cornstarch mixture. Add to pork mixture. Heat and stir for about 3 minutes until snow peas are tender-crisp and sauce is thickened. Add cashews. Stir. Serves 4.

NUTRITION INFORMATION 1 serving: 280 Calories; 12.2 g Total Fat (6.3 g Mono, 2.1 g Poly, 2.9 g Sat); 54 mg Cholesterol; 22 g Carbohydrate; 2 g Fibre; 21 g Protein; 534 mg Sodium
CHOICES 1 Fruit & Vegetable; 3 Protein; 1/2 Fat & Oil; 1 Sugar

Kid-Friendly Idea

Omit ginger and chili paste. Substitute same amount of frozen peas for the snow peas.

Maple Balsamic Tenderloin

Moist and perfectly cooked pork with sweet, tangy undertones. Great served with a salad and roasted potatoes.

Frozen concentrated apple juice, thawed	1/4 cup	60 mL
Maple (or maple-flavoured) syrup	1/4 cup	60 mL
Balsamic vinegar	3 tbsp.	50 mL
Garlic clove, minced (or 1/4 tsp., 1 mL, powder)	1	1
Pepper	1/4 tsp.	1 mL
Pork tenderloin, trimmed of fat	1 lb.	454 g

Combine first 5 ingredients in medium bowl.

Add pork. Turn until coated. Cover. Marinate in refrigerator for at least 8 hours or overnight, turning several times. Drain and discard marinade. Preheat gas barbecue to medium-high. Turn 1 burner off. Cook pork on greased grill on unlit side for 35 to 40 minutes, turning occasionally, until pork is tender and internal temperature reads 155°F (68ºC). Remove to platter. Cover with foil. Let stand for 10 minutes. Internal temperature should rise to at least 160°F (70ºC). Cut into 1 inch (2.5 cm) thick slices. Serves 4.

NUTRITION INFORMATION 1 serving: 254 Calories; 7.3 g Total Fat (3.2 g Mono, 0.8 g Poly, 2.5 g Sat); 73 mg Cholesterol; 23 g Carbohydrate; trace Fibre; 24 g Protein; 64 mg Sodium

CHOICES 1 Fruit & Vegetable; 3 Protein; 1 1/2 Sugar

Pictured on page 53.

1. Fish Parcels, page 32
2. Shrimp And Asparagus Stir-Fry, page 28
3. Parmesan Crumbed Fish, page 30

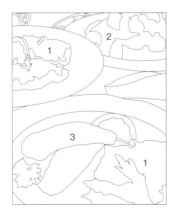

Succulent Lamb Chops

Juicy lamb chops flavoured with lime and chili. Adjust the chili sauce to suit your taste.

Lime juice	**1/4 cup**	**60 mL**
Sweet (or regular) chili sauce	**3 tbsp.**	**50 mL**
Oyster sauce	**1 tbsp.**	**15 mL**
Finely grated lime zest	**1 tsp.**	**5 mL**
Garlic clove, minced (or 1/4 tsp., 1 mL, powder)	**1**	**1**
Rack of lamb (with 8 ribs), trimmed of fat and cut into individual chops	**1**	**1**

Combine first 5 ingredients in medium bowl.

Add lamb chops. Turn until coated. Cover. Marinate in refrigerator for at least 8 hours or overnight. Drain and discard marinade. Preheat electric grill for 5 minutes or gas barbecue to medium-high. Cook chops on greased grill for about 5 minutes per side until tender and reached desired doneness. Serves 4.

NUTRITION INFORMATION 1 serving: 180 Calories; 11.5 g Total Fat (4.8 g Mono, 0.8 g Poly, 4.9 g Sat); 49 mg Cholesterol; 6 g Carbohydrate; trace Fibre; 13 g Protein; 530 mg Sodium

CHOICES 1/2 Fruit & Vegetable; 2 Protein; 1 Fat & Oil

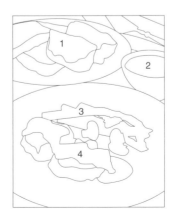

1. Mustard Dill Halibut, page 75
2. Spicy Roasted Pepper Sauce, page 113
3. Asparagus And Mushrooms, page 109
4. Peppered Lamb, page 73, with Spicy Roasted Pepper Sauce, page 113

Pepper Pork Skewers

Bright and colourful with tender pork. Serve with Crunchy Rice Salad, page 96.

Lime juice	3 tbsp.	50 mL
Apricot jam	2 tbsp.	30 mL
Dijon mustard (with whole seeds)	2 tbsp.	30 mL
Garlic clove, minced (or 1/4 tsp., 1 mL, powder)	1	1
Low-sodium soy sauce	1 tbsp.	15 mL
Pork tenderloin, trimmed of fat and cut into 1 inch (2.5 cm) cubes	1 lb.	454 g
Small red pepper, cubed	1	1
Small yellow pepper, cubed	1	1
Bamboo skewers (8 inch, 20 cm, length), soaked in water for 10 minutes	8	8
Lemon pepper	1 tsp.	5 mL

Combine first 5 ingredients in large bowl.

Add pork. Toss until coated. Cover. Marinate in refrigerator for at least 3 hours. Drain and discard marinade.

Thread pork and red and yellow peppers alternately onto skewers.

Sprinkle with lemon pepper. Preheat electric grill for 5 minutes or gas barbecue to medium-high. Cook skewers on greased grill for 15 to 20 minutes, turning occasionally, until pork is tender. Makes 8 skewers. Serves 4.

NUTRITION INFORMATION 1 serving: 101 Calories; 1.8 g Total Fat (0.7 g Mono, 0.3 g Poly, 0.5 g Sat); 33 mg Cholesterol; 7 g Carbohydrate; trace Fibre; 14 g Protein; 145 mg Sodium

CHOICES 1/2 Fruit & Vegetable; 2 Protein

Pictured on page 89.

Warm Pork Salad

Lightly coated spinach with the sweetness of dates.

Sesame (or canola) oil	1 tsp.	5 mL
Pork tenderloin, trimmed of fat and cut into 1/4 inch (6 mm) thick strips	1 lb.	454 g
Fresh spinach, stems removed (cut or torn if large), lightly packed	6 cups	1.5 L
Coarsely chopped pitted dates	1/2 cup	125 mL
Medium roma (plum) tomatoes, quartered lengthwise	3	3
MUSTARD MAYONNAISE		
Orange juice	1/4 cup	60 mL
Low-fat mayonnaise	1/4 cup	60 mL
Dijon mustard (with whole seeds)	1 tbsp.	15 mL
Salt	1/4 tsp.	1 mL
Sesame seeds, toasted (see Tip, page 63), optional	1 tbsp.	15 mL

Heat wok or large frying pan on medium-high until very hot. Add sesame oil. Add pork. Stir-fry for about 5 minutes until tender and lightly browned. Transfer to large bowl.

Add next 3 ingredients. Toss gently.

Mustard Mayonnaise: Combine first 4 ingredients in jar with tight-fitting lid. Shake well. Makes about 1/2 cup (125 mL) mayonnaise. Drizzle over salad. Toss.

Sprinkle with sesame seeds. Makes about 9 1/2 cups (2.4 L). Serves 6.

NUTRITION INFORMATION 1 serving: 224 Calories; 9.3 g Total Fat (4.3 g Mono, 2.1 g Poly, 2.1 g Sat); 48 mg Cholesterol; 19 g Carbohydrate; 4 g Fibre; 18 g Protein; 291 mg Sodium

CHOICES 1 1/2 Fruit & Vegetable; 2 1/2 Protein; 1/2 Fat & Oil

Pictured on page 53.

Kid-Friendly Idea

Substitute same amount of chopped romaine lettuce for the spinach. Omit dates.

NUTRITION INFORMATION 1 cup (250 mL): 118 Calories; 6.1 g Total Fat (2.9 g Mono, 1.4 g Poly, 1.4 g Sat); 2 mg Cholesterol; 4 g Carbohydrate; 1 g Fibre; 12 g Protein; 166 mg Sodium

CHOICES 1/2 Fruit & Vegetable; 1 1/2 Protein; 1/2 Fat & Oil

Artichoke And Ham Pie

An attractive meat pie with red peppers and artichokes peeking through. Great for brunch, lunch or light dinner. Prepare the day before and chill for up to 24 hours before baking.

Whole wheat bread slices (with crusts), cut into 1 inch (2.5 cm) squares	4	4
Lean deli ham, chopped (about 1 cup, 250 mL)	5 oz.	140 g
Can of artichoke hearts, drained and chopped	14 oz.	398 mL
Diced roasted red peppers (see Note)	1/4 cup	60 mL
Finely grated fresh Parmesan cheese	1/3 cup	75 mL
Can of skim evaporated milk	13 1/2 oz.	385 mL
Non-fat creamed cottage cheese	1/2 cup	125 mL
Large eggs	4	4
Egg whites (large)	2	2
All-purpose flour	1 tbsp.	15 mL
Garlic cloves, halved (or 3/4 tsp., 4 mL, powder)	3	3
Ground nutmeg	1/8 tsp.	0.5 mL
Hard margarine (or butter), melted (optional)	1 tbsp.	15 mL
Paprika, sprinkle		
Pepper, sprinkle		

Spray 10 inch (25 cm) pie plate or 9 inch (22 cm) deep-dish pie plate with cooking spray. Layer first 5 ingredients in plate in order given.

Process next 7 ingredients in blender or food processor for several seconds until almost smooth. Pour over layers. Cover. Chill for at least 6 hours.

Drizzle margarine over top. Sprinkle with paprika and pepper. Bake, uncovered, in 375°F (190°C) oven for 55 to 60 minutes until edge is golden and pie is evenly puffed across centre. Let stand for 10 minutes. Cuts into 6 wedges.

NUTRITION INFORMATION 1 wedge: 256 Calories; 7.1 g Total Fat (2.6 g Mono, 0.8 g Poly, 2.8 g Sat); 161 mg Cholesterol; 24 g Carbohydrate; 3 g Fibre; 25 g Protein; 800 mg Sodium

CHOICES 1/2 Starch; 1/2 Fruit & Vegetable; 1 1/2 Milk; 2 1/2 Protein

Note: Roasted red peppers are available in jars in most grocery stores. Drain well.

Stuffed Zucchini

These "boats" are always so appealing in the late summer when zucchini are in abundance. Mushrooms and cheese complement the zucchini.

Large zucchini (with peel), about 12 oz., 340 g	2	2
Olive (or canola) oil	1 tsp.	5 mL
Olive (or canola) oil	2 tsp.	10 mL
Chopped fresh brown (or white) mushrooms	2 cups	500 mL
Garlic clove, minced (or 1/4 tsp., 1 mL, powder)	1	1
Lemon pepper	1/2 tsp.	2 mL
Grated part-skim mozzarella cheese	3/4 cup	175 mL
Finely chopped fresh oregano (or marjoram) or 3/4 tsp. (4 mL), dried	1 tbsp.	15 mL
Crumbled low-fat feta cheese (about 1 3/4 oz., 50 g)	1/4 cup	60 mL

Slice off both ends of zucchini. Cut in half lengthwise. Remove and reserve flesh using small spoon, leaving 1/4 inch (6 mm) thick shell. Brush cut sides of zucchini lightly with first amount of olive oil. Be sure to use it all. Place, cut side up, in ungreased shallow baking pan. Bake in 400°F (205°C) oven for about 15 minutes until soft when squeezed lightly.

Heat second amount of olive oil in large non-stick frying pan on medium. Add reserved zucchini and next 3 ingredients. Stir. Cook for about 10 minutes, stirring often, until liquid is evaporated. Transfer to medium bowl. Cool for 10 minutes.

Add mozzarella cheese and oregano. Makes about 1 cup (250 mL) stuffing. Divide and stuff into each zucchini shell.

Divide and sprinkle feta cheese over stuffing. Bake, uncovered, in 400°F (205°C) oven for about 15 minutes until heated through. Makes 4 stuffed zucchini.

NUTRITION INFORMATION 1 stuffed zucchini: 140 Calories; 9.6 g Total Fat (3.6 g Mono, 1.3 g Poly, 4.1 g Sat); 18 mg Cholesterol; 6 g Carbohydrate; 2 g Fibre; 9 g Protein; 149 mg Sodium

CHOICES 1/2 Fruit & Vegetable; 1 Protein; 1 1/2 Fat & Oil

Kid-Friendly Idea

Substitute same amount of grated light Monterey Jack cheese for the feta cheese.

NUTRITION INFORMATION 1 stuffed zucchini: 141 Calories; 9.8 g Total Fat (3.8 g Mono, 1.3 g Poly, 4.1 g Sat); 20 mg Cholesterol; 5 g Carbohydrate; 2 g Fibre; 9 g Protein; 153 mg Sodium

CHOICES 1/2 Fruit & Vegetable; 1 Protein; 1 1/2 Fat & Oil

Vegetable Lasagne

Make this delicious dish the day before and pop it in the oven after work. Serve with a tossed green salad and fresh tomatoes.

Whole wheat lasagna noodles	6	6
Boiling water	12 cups	3 L
Salt	2 tsp.	10 mL
Olive (or canola) oil	1 tbsp.	15 mL
Broccoli slaw (or shredded cabbage with carrot)	2 cups	500 mL
Diced zucchini (with peel)	2 cups	500 mL
Sliced fresh brown (or white) mushrooms	2 cups	500 mL
Coarsely grated carrot	3/4 cup	175 mL
Medium onion, chopped	1	1
Garlic cloves, minced (or 1/2 tsp., 2 mL, powder), optional	2	2
Can of stewed tomatoes (with juice), chopped	14 oz.	398 mL
Tomato paste (see Tip, page 43)	2 tbsp.	30 mL
Chopped fresh basil (or 2 1/4 tsp., 11 mL, dried)	3 tbsp.	50 mL
Chopped fresh parsley (or 2 1/4 tsp., 11 mL, flakes)	3 tbsp.	50 mL
Pepper, generous sprinkle		
Tub of non-fat creamed cottage cheese	17 1/2 oz.	500 g
Large eggs	2	2
Fresh spinach, stems removed, lightly packed	2 cups	500 mL
Finely grated fresh Parmesan cheese	1/3 cup	75 mL
Skim evaporated milk	2/3 cup	150 mL
Garlic and herb no-salt seasoning (such as Mrs. Dash)	1 tsp.	5 mL
Grated part-skim mozzarella cheese	1 cup	250 mL

Cook noodles in boiling water and salt in large uncovered pot or Dutch oven for 10 minutes, stirring often. Noodles will still be firm. Drain. Rinse with cold water. Set aside.

Heat wok or large frying pan on medium-high until very hot. Add olive oil. Add next 6 ingredients. Stir-fry for 5 minutes. Cook, uncovered, for 4 to 5 minutes, stirring occasionally, until vegetables are soft and liquid is evaporated.

Add next 5 ingredients. Stir. Remove from heat. Measure 1 cup (250 mL) into greased 9 x 13 inch (22 x 33 cm) dish. Spread thinly. Lay 3 noodles over top. Spread 1/2 of remaining sauce over top.

(continued on next page)

Place next 6 ingredients in blender. Pulse with on/off motion, scraping down sides as necessary, until smooth. Pour about 1 3/4 cups (425 mL) over tomato mixture. Spread evenly. Layer remaining noodles, remaining tomato mixture and cottage cheese mixture, in order given, over top.

Sprinkle with mozzarella cheese. Cover tightly with greased foil. Bake in 325°F (160°C) oven for 45 minutes. Remove foil. Bake at 375°F (190°C) for about 15 minutes until edges are golden. Let stand on wire rack for 15 minutes before cutting. Serves 6.

NUTRITION INFORMATION 1 serving: 355 Calories; 10 g Total Fat (3.9 g Mono, 0.9 g Poly, 4.2 g Sat); 89 mg Cholesterol; 36 g Carbohydrate; 6 g Fibre; 33 g Protein; 629 mg Sodium

CHOICES 1 Starch; 1 1/2 Fruit & Vegetable; 1/2 Milk; 4 Protein

Pictured on page 54.

Kid-Friendly Idea

Finely chop all the vegetables so there aren't any large pieces. Reduce amount of basil.

To store tomato paste when recipe doesn't call for a whole can, freeze unopened can for 30 minutes. Open both ends and push contents through, slicing off only what you need. Freeze remaining tomato paste in resealable freezer bag for future use.

Bows And Fresh Vegetables

A creamy garlic sauce coats colourful vegetables and bow pasta. Have your vegetables cut before cooking the pasta. The flavours are enhanced by a pinch of salt, if your diet permits.

Medium bow pasta (about 3 cups, 750 mL)	**8 oz.**	**225 g**
Boiling water	**12 cups**	**3 L**
Salt	**1 tbsp.**	**15 mL**
Broccoli florets	**1 cup**	**250 mL**
Chopped fresh asparagus, trimmed of tough ends before chopping	**1 cup**	**250 mL**
Small red pepper, seeds and ribs removed, diced	**1**	**1**
Fresh snow peas	**1 cup**	**250 mL**
Skim milk	**1 1/2 cups**	**375 mL**
All-purpose flour	**2 tbsp.**	**30 mL**
Garlic powder	**1/4 tsp.**	**1 mL**
Salt (optional)	**1/4 tsp.**	**1 mL**
Grated part-skim mozzarella cheese	**1/2 cup**	**125 mL**
Chopped fresh parsley (or 3/4 tsp., 4 mL, flakes)	**1 tbsp.**	**15 mL**
Finely grated fresh Parmesan cheese	**1 tbsp.**	**15 mL**
Freshly ground pepper, for garnish		

Cook pasta in boiling water and salt in large uncovered pot or Dutch oven for 6 minutes, stirring occasionally. Do not drain.

Add broccoli and asparagus. Bring to a boil. Cook, uncovered, for 2 minutes.

Add red pepper and snow peas. Bring to a boil. Cook, uncovered, for about 3 minutes until pasta is tender but firm. Drain. Return to pot. Cover to keep warm.

Slowly stir milk into flour in medium saucepan until smooth. Add garlic powder and salt. Cook and stir on medium for about 10 minutes, until boiling and thickened.

Add mozzarella cheese. Stir until melted. Pour over pasta mixture. Toss. Transfer to warm serving bowl.

Sprinkle parsley, Parmesan cheese and pepper over top just before serving. Makes 7 cups (1.75 L). Serves 4 to 6.

NUTRITION INFORMATION 1 serving: 339 Calories; 4.3 g Total Fat (1 g Mono, 0.6 g Poly, 2.2 g Sat); 12 mg Cholesterol; 57 g Carbohydrate; 4 g Fibre; 18 g Protein; 165 mg Sodium

CHOICES 3 Starch; 1/2 Fruit & Vegetable; 1/2 Milk; 1 Protein

Pictured on front cover.

(continued on next page)

Kid-Friendly Idea

Use your child's favourite vegetables instead of the broccoli, asparagus, red pepper and/or snow peas. Remember to add firmer vegetables after pasta has cooked for 6 minutes and softer vegetables nearer the end of cooking time.

Lemon Asparagus Penne

Lots of lemony fresh sauce. Very satisfying dish.

Whole wheat penne pasta (about 10 1/2 oz., 300 g)	2 2/3 cups	650 mL
Boiling water	8 cups	2 L
Salt	2 tsp.	10 mL
Part-skim ricotta cheese (about 6 1/2 oz., 184 g)	3/4 cup	175 mL
Finely grated lemon zest	1 tbsp.	15 mL
Skim evaporated milk	1/2 cup	125 mL
Olive (or canola) oil	1 tbsp.	15 mL
Fresh asparagus, trimmed of tough ends and cut into 1 inch (2.5 cm) pieces	1 1/2 lbs.	680 g
Garlic cloves, minced (or 3/4 tsp., 4 mL, powder)	3	3
Green onions, cut diagonally into 1 inch (2.5 cm) pieces	6	6
Finely grated fresh Parmesan cheese	2 tbsp.	30 mL
Freshly ground pepper, for garnish		

Cook pasta in boiling water and salt in large uncovered pot or Dutch oven for 10 to 12 minutes, stirring occasionally, until tender but firm. Drain, reserving 3/4 cup (175 mL) cooking water. Rinse pasta with hot water. Drain well. Return to pot.

Put ricotta cheese and lemon zest into blender or food processor. Add reserved hot cooking water and evaporated milk. Process until smooth.

Heat olive oil in large frying pan on medium. Add asparagus, garlic and green onion. Stir. Cover. Cook for about 5 minutes, shaking pan several times, until asparagus is tender-crisp and starting to brown. Add ricotta cheese mixture. Stir for about 2 minutes until heated through. Add to pasta. Toss well. Transfer to serving bowl.

Sprinkle with Parmesan cheese and pepper. Makes 8 cups (2 L). Serves 4.

NUTRITION INFORMATION 1 serving: 376 Calories; 9.4 g Total Fat (4.1 g Mono, 0.9 g Poly, 3.7 g Sat); 19 mg Cholesterol; 57 g Carbohydrate; 7 g Fibre; 21 g Protein; 168 mg Sodium

CHOICES 2 1/2 Starch; 1/2 Fruit & Vegetable; 1 Milk; 1 1/2 Protein; 1 Fat & Oil

Spinach And Cheese Roll

Lovely golden, flaky pastry and subtle, tangy feta flavour. Serve with a crisp lettuce and tomato salad.

Olive (or canola) oil	2 tsp.	10 mL
Finely chopped onion	1 cup	250 mL
Garlic cloves, minced (or 1 tsp., 5 mL, powder)	4	4
Boxes of frozen chopped spinach (10 oz., 300 g, each), thawed and squeezed dry	2	2
Lemon pepper	1/2 tsp.	2 mL
Ground nutmeg	1/4 tsp.	1 mL
Part-skim ricotta cheese, drained (about 4 1/2 oz., 127 g)	1/2 cup	125 mL
Crumbled low-fat feta cheese (about 3 1/2 oz., 100 g)	1/2 cup	125 mL
Chopped fresh parsley (or 2 1/4 tsp., 11 mL, flakes)	3 tbsp.	50 mL
Frozen phyllo pastry sheets, thawed according to package directions	6	6
ROASTED PEPPER SAUCE		
Jar of roasted red peppers, drained and blotted dry	13 oz.	370 mL
Balsamic vinegar	1 tbsp.	15 mL
Brown sugar, packed	1 tsp.	5 mL
Lemon pepper	1/4 tsp.	1 mL

Heat olive oil in large non-stick frying pan on medium. Add onion and garlic. Cook for about 5 minutes, stirring often, until onion is softened.

Chop spinach into small pieces. Add to onion mixture. Add lemon pepper and nutmeg. Stir. Cook for 1 to 2 minutes, stirring often, until heated through and liquid is evaporated. Transfer to medium bowl. Cool to room temperature.

Add ricotta cheese, feta cheese and parsley. Stir well.

Lay tea towel, short end closest to you, on work surface. Place 1 phyllo sheet, short end closest to you, on tea towel. Cover remaining sheets with damp tea towel to prevent drying out. Lightly spray first sheet with cooking spray. Place second sheet on top of first. Working quickly, lightly spray with cooking spray. Repeat layering and spraying with remaining sheets. Mound spinach filling evenly along short end of pastry closest to you, 6 inches (15 cm) from bottom edge, leaving about 1 inch (2.5 cm) on either side. Fold bottom edge of sheets up and over filling. Roll firmly to enclose filling, using tea towel as a guide. Pack any loose filling back into roll. Do not tuck in sides. Place, seam-side down, on greased baking sheet with sides. Spray with cooking spray. Bake in 400°F (205ºC) oven for 15 to 20 minutes until golden brown. Cut into twelve 1 inch (2.5 cm) slices.

(continued on next page)

Roasted Pepper Sauce: Process all 4 ingredients in blender until smooth. Pour into medium saucepan. Heat on medium, stirring occasionally, until boiling. Reduce heat to medium-low. Simmer, uncovered, for 5 minutes. Makes 3/4 cup (175 mL) sauce. Spoon sauce over slices. Serves 6.

NUTRITION INFORMATION 1 serving: 183 Calories; 8.6 g Total Fat (2.8 g Mono, 1.1 g Poly, 4.2 g Sat); 17 mg Cholesterol; 19 g Carbohydrate; 2 g Fibre; 9 g Protein; 540 mg Sodium

CHOICES 1 Starch; 1 Protein; 1 Fat & Oil

Pictured on front cover.

Kid-Friendly Idea

Substitute about 1 1/2 cups (375 mL) of your child's favourite cooked vegetables for the spinach. Replace feta cheese with light sharp Cheddar cheese.

NUTRITION INFORMATION 1 serving: 194 Calories; 9.1 g Total Fat (3.1 g Mono, 1.1 g Poly, 4.3 g Sat); 21 mg Cholesterol; 21 g Carbohydrate; 2 g Fibre; 8 g Protein; 539 mg Sodium

CHOICES 1 Starch; 1/2 Fruit & Vegetable; 1 Protein; 1 Fat & Oil

Roasted Red Pepper Pizza

Delicious, easy-to-prepare pizza with a flavourful topping.

Prebaked pizza crust (12 inch, 30 cm, diameter), such as Boboli	**1**	**1**
Pizza sauce	**1/3 cup**	**75 mL**
Chopped roasted red peppers	**1 cup**	**250 mL**
Fresh spinach, stems removed, lightly packed	**1 cup**	**250 mL**
Thinly sliced red onion	**1 cup**	**250 mL**
Chopped fresh basil (or 1 1/2 tsp., 7 mL, dried)	**2 tbsp.**	**30 mL**
Crumbled low-fat feta cheese (about 2 oz., 57 g)	**1/3 cup**	**75 mL**
Finely grated fresh Parmesan cheese	**3 tbsp.**	**50 mL**

Place pizza crust on ungreased 12 inch (30 cm) pizza pan or baking sheet. Spread pizza sauce evenly over crust.

Layer remaining 6 ingredients, in order given, over sauce. Bake on lowest rack in 475°F (240ºC) oven for about 20 minutes until crust is browned. Cuts into 8 wedges.

NUTRITION INFORMATION 1 wedge: 145 Calories; 3.9 g Total Fat (0.8 g Mono, 0.2 g Poly, 1.6 g Sat); 5 mg Cholesterol; 21 g Carbohydrate; 1 g Fibre; 6 g Protein; 304 mg Sodium

CHOICES 1 Starch; 1/2 Fruit & Vegetable; 1/2 Protein; 1/2 Fat & Oil

Pictured on page 54.

Chicken Cacciatore

Tender chicken and fresh vegetables rest in a rich, red tomato sauce. Serve the excess sauce over pasta. Delicious!

Ingredient	Imperial	Metric
All-purpose flour	2 tbsp.	30 mL
Paprika	1/2 tsp.	2 mL
Salt	1/4 tsp.	1 mL
Pepper	1/4 tsp.	1 mL
Boneless, skinless chicken thighs, halved	1 lb.	454 g
Chopped onion	3/4 cup	175 mL
Chopped red pepper	1/2 cup	125 mL
Chopped green pepper	1/2 cup	125 mL
Garlic cloves, minced (or 1/2 tsp., 2 mL, powder)	2	2
Can of diced tomatoes (with juice)	28 oz.	796 mL
Sliced fresh white mushrooms	2 cups	500 mL
Tomato paste (see Tip, page 43)	1/4 cup	60 mL
Balsamic vinegar	1 tbsp.	15 mL
Granulated sugar	1/2 tsp.	2 mL

Combine first 4 ingredients in large plastic bag.

Add chicken. Seal. Toss until coated. Shake excess flour mixture from chicken. Transfer to 3 quart (3 L) casserole. Cover. Microwave on high (100%) for 3 minutes. Turn chicken. Cover. Microwave on high (100%) for 2 to 3 minutes until no longer pink inside. Transfer chicken to plate.

Put next 4 ingredients into same casserole. Stir. Cover. Microwave on high (100%) for 5 to 7 minutes until vegetables are tender. Stir.

Add chicken and remaining 5 ingredients. Stir. Cover. Microwave on high (100%) for 5 minutes. Stir. Cover. Microwave for 10 to 12 minutes until chicken is tender. Serves 4.

NUTRITION INFORMATION 1 serving: 255 Calories; 7.1 g Total Fat (2 g Mono, 2 g Poly, 1.7 g Sat); 94 mg Cholesterol; 23 g Carbohydrate; 4 g Fibre; 26 g Protein; 492 mg Sodium

CHOICES 2 Fruit & Vegetable; 3 1/2 Protein

Pictured on page 71.

Kid-Friendly Idea

Substitute same amount of white vinegar for the balsamic.

Turkey In Curry Sauce

A rich, yellow curry sauce coats chunks of turkey and soft mango.

Chopped onion	1 cup	250 mL
Flake coconut	2 tbsp.	30 mL
Canola oil	2 tsp.	10 mL
Curry powder	2 tsp.	10 mL
Chili powder	1/4 tsp.	1 mL
Ground cinnamon	1/4 tsp.	1 mL
All-purpose flour	2 tsp.	10 mL
2% evaporated milk	1 cup	250 mL
Turkey breast, diced	1 lb.	454 g
Can of sliced mangos (or peaches) in light syrup, drained and diced **Salt, sprinkle (optional)**	14 oz.	398 mL
Hot cooked jasmine (or other) rice (about 2 cups, 500 mL, uncooked)	4 cups	1 L

Put first 6 ingredients into ungreased 1 1/2 quart (1.5 L) casserole. Stir. Cover. Microwave on high (100%) for 3 minutes, stirring twice.

Sprinkle flour over onion mixture. Stir. Cover. Microwave on high (100%) for about 1 minute until onion is softened.

Add evaporated milk. Stir. Cover. Microwave on high (100%) for 1 to 2 minutes until boiling and slightly thickened.

Add turkey. Stir until coated. Cover. Microwave on high (100%) for 4 minutes, stirring once at halftime.

Add mangos. Stir. Cover. Microwave on medium (50%) for 3 minutes, stirring once at halftime. Let stand for 2 minutes. Makes about 3 3/4 cups (925 mL).

Spoon over rice. Serves 4.

NUTRITION INFORMATION 1 serving: 524 Calories; 7.2 g Total Fat (2.2 g Mono, 1.2 g Poly, 3.1 g Sat); 99 mg Cholesterol; 68 g Carbohydrate; 3 g Fibre; 45 g Protein; 144 mg Sodium

CHOICES 3 1/2 Starch; 1 Fruit & Vegetable; 1 Milk; 4 1/2 Protein

To ensure even cooking in a microwave, rotate dish half a turn halfway through cooking time.

Asian Rice Bowl

A wonderful, fresh-tasting dish with a variety of crunchy vegetables and a lingering heat.

Brown converted rice	1 cup	250 mL
Hot water	2 cups	500 mL
Finely chopped onion	1/2 cup	125 mL
Sweet (or regular) chili sauce	1 tbsp.	15 mL
Garlic cloves, minced (or 1/2 tsp., 2 mL, powder)	2	2
Dried crushed chilies (optional)	1/4 tsp.	1 mL
Lean ground chicken	8 oz.	225 g
Green onions, sliced	4	4
Dry sherry	1 tbsp.	15 mL
Low-sodium soy sauce	2 tbsp.	30 mL
Rice vinegar (or lemon juice)	4 tsp.	20 mL
Cornstarch	2 tsp.	10 mL
Fresh (or frozen, thawed) cooked salad shrimp	4 oz.	113 g
Bean sprouts	2 cups	500 mL
Green onion, sliced	1	1
Julienned English cucumber (with peel)	1/4 cup	60 mL
Finely chopped roasted unsalted peanuts (optional)	2 tbsp.	30 mL

Place rice and hot water in ungreased 2 quart (2 L) casserole. Stir. Cover. Microwave on high (100%) for 12 minutes. Let stand for 10 minutes.

Combine next 4 ingredients in ungreased 1 quart (1 L) casserole. Cover. Microwave on high (100%) for 2 minutes. Stir.

Add ground chicken, first amount of green onion and sherry. Stir. Cover. Microwave on high (100%) for 4 minutes, stirring once at halftime.

Stir soy sauce and vinegar into cornstarch in small cup until smooth. Stir into chicken mixture. Cover. Microwave on high (100%) for about 1 minute until boiling and slightly thickened. Add to rice. Stir. Add shrimp and bean sprouts. Stir. Cover. Microwave on high (100%) for about 2 minutes until heated through. Divide and spoon into 4 individual bowls.

Divide and top with second amount of green onion, cucumber and peanuts. Serves 4.

NUTRITION INFORMATION 1 serving: 323 Calories; 3.6 g Total Fat (1.1 g Mono, 1.1 g Poly, 0.8 g Sat); 94 mg Cholesterol; 48 g Carbohydrate; 4 g Fibre; 24 g Protein; 417 mg Sodium

CHOICES 3 Starch; 2 1/2 Protein

(continued on next page)

Kid-Friendly Idea

Substitute long grain white rice for the brown converted rice. Omit chili sauce, dried crushed chilies and green onions. Substitute one 4 oz. (113 g) chicken breast half, diced, for the shrimp.

NUTRITION INFORMATION 1 serving: 353 Calories; 5.1g Total Fat (2 g Mono, 1.4 g Poly, 1.1 g Sat); 63 mg Cholesterol; 48 g Carbohydrate; 2 g Fibre; 27 g Protein; 296 mg Sodium

CHOICES 3 Starch; 3 Protein

Chicken Stroganoff

A savoury variation which uses cream cheese instead of sour cream.

Sliced fresh white mushrooms	2 cups	500 mL
Thinly sliced onion	1 cup	250 mL
Canola oil	2 tsp.	10 mL
Paprika	1/2 tsp.	2 mL
Garlic clove, minced (or 1/4 tsp., 1 mL, powder)	1	1
Boneless, skinless chicken thighs, cut into thin strips	1 lb.	454 g
Tomato paste (see Tip, page 43)	1/4 cup	60 mL
Salt, sprinkle		
Pepper	1/4 tsp.	1 mL
Chopped light cream cheese, softened	1/4 cup	60 mL
Low-sodium prepared chicken broth	1/4 cup	60 mL
Cornstarch	2 tsp.	10 mL

Combine first 5 ingredients in ungreased 2 quart (2 L) casserole. Cover. Microwave on high (100%) for 8 minutes, stirring once at halftime.

Add next 4 ingredients. Stir. Cover. Microwave on high (100%) for about 8 minutes, stirring once at halftime, until chicken is tender. Stir.

Add cream cheese. Stir.

Stir broth into cornstarch in small bowl until smooth. Add to chicken mixture. Stir. Cover. Microwave on high (100%) for 1 minute. Stir. Microwave on high (100%) for about 1 minute until hot and cheese is melted. Makes about 3 cups (750 mL). Serves 4.

NUTRITION INFORMATION 1 serving: 184 Calories; 9.1 g Total Fat (3.4 g Mono, 1.8 g Poly, 2.8 g Sat); 61 mg Cholesterol; 11 g Carbohydrate; 2 g Fibre; 16 g Protein; 163 mg Sodium

CHOICES 1 Fruit & Vegetable; 2 Protein; 1/2 Fat & Oil

Roasted Lamb Rack

Succulent lamb chops covered with a glossy honey garlic sauce. These are quick and so easy to prepare.

Liquid honey	**2 tbsp.**	**30 mL**
Low-sodium soy sauce	**1 tbsp.**	**15 mL**
Dried rosemary	**1 tsp.**	**5 mL**
Garlic powder	**1/2 tsp.**	**2 mL**
Pepper	**1/4 tsp.**	**1 mL**
Rack of lamb (with 8 ribs), trimmed of fat	**13 oz.**	**370 g**

Combine first 5 ingredients in small bowl.

Place lamb rack, meat-side up, in shallow microwave-safe dish. Brush with honey mixture. Turn over. Microwave, uncovered, on high (100%) for 5 minutes. Turn over. Microwave on high (100%) for 2 to 4 minutes until desired doneness or meat thermometer registers 140°F to 160°F (60°C to 70°C) when inserted into thickest part of meat. Cover. Let stand for 5 minutes. Cut rack into individual chops. Makes 8 chops. Serves 4.

NUTRITION INFORMATION 1 serving: 206 Calories; 13 g Total Fat (5.3 g Mono, 1 g Poly, 5.6 g Sat); 52 mg Cholesterol; 10 g Carbohydrate; trace Fibre; 13 g Protein; 158 mg Sodium

CHOICES 1 1/2 Protein; 1 1/2 Fat & Oil; 1 Sugar

1. Warm Pork Salad, page 39
2. Apple Cranberry Chutney, page 117
3. Maple Balsamic Tenderloin, page 34
4. Spinach Mushroom Rice, page 93

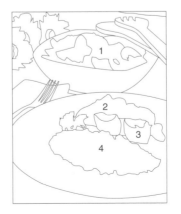

Mustard Honey Salmon

Moist, perfectly cooked salmon with a delicious honey mustard glaze. Serve with a crisp green salad or Easy Couscous, page 92.

Dijon mustard	**2 tbsp.**	**30 mL**
Chopped fresh parsley (or 1 1/2 tsp., 7 mL, flakes)	**2 tbsp.**	**30 mL**
Liquid honey	**2 tbsp.**	**30 mL**
Garlic salt	**1/2 tsp.**	**2 mL**
Salmon fillets (about 3/4 inch, 2 cm, thick), 5 oz. (140 g) each	**4**	**4**

Combine first 4 ingredients in small bowl.

Place salmon in shallow microwave-safe dish. Brush mustard mixture over salmon. Cover. Microwave on high (100%) for 4 to 5 minutes until salmon flakes easily when tested with fork. Let stand for 2 minutes. Serves 4.

NUTRITION INFORMATION 1 serving: 242 Calories; 9.5 g Total Fat (3.1 g Mono, 3.9 g Poly, 1.5 g Sat); 78 mg Cholesterol; 9 g Carbohydrate; trace Fibre; 29 g Protein; 317 mg Sodium

CHOICES 4 Protein; 1 Sugar

1. Vegetable Lasagne, page 42
2. Roasted Red Pepper Pizza, page 47

Pasta And Cheese Supper

A warm, cheesy sauce coats perfectly cooked whole wheat pasta. Serve with a fresh garden salad.

Whole wheat rotini (or fusilli) pasta (about 8 oz., 225 g)	2 2/3 cups	650 mL
Boiling water	10 cups	2.5 L
Salt	2 tsp.	10 mL
Olive (or canola) oil	1 tbsp.	15 mL
Finely chopped onion	2/3 cup	150 mL
All-purpose flour	1/4 cup	60 mL
Dry mustard	1/2 tsp.	2 mL
Salt	1/4 tsp.	1 mL
Pepper, sprinkle		
Milk	2 cups	500 mL
Creamed non-fat cottage cheese, mashed (or processed) until almost smooth	1 cup	250 mL
Grated light sharp Cheddar cheese	1 cup	250 mL
Grated part-skim mozzarella cheese	1 cup	250 mL

Cook pasta in boiling water and salt in large uncovered pot or Dutch oven for 10 to 12 minutes, stirring occasionally, until tender but firm. Drain. Rinse with cold water. Drain well. Return to pot to keep warm.

Combine olive oil and onion in ungreased 3 quart (3 L) casserole. Cover. Microwave on high (100%) for about 4 minutes, stirring once at halftime, until onion is softened.

Add next 4 ingredients. Stir. Gradually whisk in milk. Cover. Microwave on medium (50%) for 4 minutes. Stir with whisk. Cover. Microwave on medium (50%) for 8 to 10 minutes, stirring twice, until boiling and thickened.

Add cottage cheese, Cheddar cheese and mozzarella cheese. Stir well. Add pasta. Toss. Spread evenly. Cover. Microwave on medium (50%) for 10 minutes. Let stand for 2 minutes before serving. Makes 6 cups (1.5 L). Serves 4.

NUTRITION INFORMATION 1 serving: 546 Calories; 16.8 Total Fat (6.3 g Mono, 1 g Poly, 8.4 g Sat); 41 mg Cholesterol; 5 g Fibre; 40 g Protein; 665 mg Sodium

CHOICES 3 Starch; 1/2 Fruit & Vegetable; 1 Milk; 4 Protein; 1/2 Fat & Oil

Beef And Tomato Stew

A vibrant, saucy stew with a wonderful variety of fresh flavours and textures. A quick, easy dish that goes well with a salad or hot vegetables.

Thinly sliced onion	1 1/2 cups	375 mL
Garlic cloves, minced (or 1/2 tsp., 2 mL, powder)	2	2
Olive (or canola) oil	2 tsp.	10 mL
Beef sirloin tip steak, cut into 2 inch (5 cm) thick strips	3/4 lb.	340 g
Water	1/2 cup	125 mL
All-purpose flour	1 1/2 tbsp.	25 mL
Can of stewed tomatoes (with juice), broken up	14 oz.	398 mL
Paprika (Hungarian is best)	2 tsp.	10 mL
Low-sodium beef bouillon powder	1 tsp.	5 mL
Granulated sugar	1 tsp.	5 mL
Dried marjoram	1/2 tsp.	2 mL
Worcestershire sauce	1/2 tsp.	2 mL
Pepper	1/4 tsp.	1 mL
Light sour cream	2 tbsp.	30 mL
Balsamic vinegar	1 1/2 tsp.	7 mL

Combine onion, garlic and olive oil in ungreased 2 quart (2 L) casserole. Cover. Microwave on high (100%) for about 4 minutes, stirring once at halftime, until onion is softened.

Add beef. Stir. Cover. Microwave on high (100%) for 3 minutes.

Stir water into flour in medium bowl until smooth. Add next 7 ingredients. Stir. Add to beef mixture. Stir. Cover. Microwave on medium (50%) for 10 to 12 minutes, stirring once at halftime, until sauce is boiling and thickened.

Add sour cream and vinegar. Stir. Makes 4 cups (1 L). Serves 4.

NUTRITION INFORMATION 1 serving: 208 Calories; 6.5 g Total Fat (3.4 g Mono, 0.6 g Poly, 2.2 g Sat); 42 mg Cholesterol; 17 g Carbohydrate; 3 g Fibre; 21 g Protein; 413 mg Sodium

CHOICES 1 1/2 Fruit & Vegetables; 2 1/2 Protein

Kid-Friendly Idea

Substitute same amount of white vinegar for the balsamic.

Apricot Beef Casserole

A richly flavoured gravy coats tender, moist strips of beef. Perfect served with couscous, rice or noodles.

Canola oil	2 tsp.	10 mL
Thinly sliced onion	1 cup	250 mL
All-purpose flour	1 tbsp.	15 mL
Curry powder	2 tsp.	10 mL
Ground cinnamon	1/4 tsp.	1 mL
Pepper	1/4 tsp.	1 mL
Beef sirloin tip (or round) steak, cut into thin strips	1 lb.	454 g
Liquid gravy browner	1/2 tsp.	2 mL
Apricot nectar	3/4 cup	175 mL
Chopped dried apricots	1/2 cup	125 mL
Worcestershire sauce	1 tsp.	5 mL
Chopped fresh parsley (or 1 1/2 tsp., 7 mL, flakes)	2 tbsp.	30 mL
Salt, sprinkle		

Combine canola oil and onion in ungreased 2 quart (2 L) casserole. Cover. Microwave on high (100%) for about 5 minutes, stirring once at halftime, until onion is softened. Set aside.

Combine next 4 ingredients in large plastic bag.

Add beef. Seal. Toss until coated. Remove beef. Add to onion. Stir. Drizzle with gravy browner. Stir. Cover. Microwave on high (100%) for 3 minutes. Stir.

Add nectar, apricots and Worcestershire sauce. Stir. Cover. Microwave on medium (50%) for about 20 minutes, stirring once at halftime, until beef is tender.

Sprinkle with parsley and salt. Stir. Makes about 2 1/2 cups (625 mL). Serves 4.

NUTRITION INFORMATION 1 serving: 263 Calories; 7.1 g Total Fat (3.2 g Mono, 1 g Poly, 1.7 g Sat); 54 mg Cholesterol; 24 g Carbohydrate; 3 g Fibre; 26 g Protein; 114 mg Sodium

CHOICES 2 Fruit & Vegetable; 3 1/2 Protein

Chicken Paprikash

Bite-size chunks of chicken rest in a tangy tomato sauce flavoured with paprika and green pepper.
An easy-to-prepare dish that can be on the table in 30 minutes.

Broad yolk-free egg noodles (about 5 cups, 1.25 mL)	8 oz.	225 g
Boiling water	8 cups	2 L
Salt	2 tsp.	10 mL
Chopped onion	1/2 cup	125 mL
Diced green pepper	1/2 cup	125 mL
Olive (or canola) oil	2 tsp.	10 mL
Garlic cloves, minced (or 1/2 tsp., 2 mL, powder)	2	2
Boneless, skinless chicken breast halves, cut into 1 inch (2.5 cm) cubes	1 lb.	454 g
Can of tomato sauce	7 1/2 oz.	213 mL
Real bacon bits (or 2 slices cooked crisp and crumbled)	2 tbsp.	30 mL
Paprika (Hungarian is best)	1 tbsp.	15 mL
Pepper	1/2 tsp.	2 mL
Light sour cream	1/2 cup	125 mL
All-purpose flour	2 tsp.	10 mL

Cook noodles in boiling water and salt in large uncovered pot or Dutch oven for 6 to 7 minutes, stirring occasionally, until tender but firm. Drain. Cover to keep warm.

Combine next 4 ingredients in ungreased 2 quart (2 L) casserole. Cover. Microwave on high (100%) for about 4 minutes, stirring once at halftime, until onion is softened.

Add next 5 ingredients. Stir. Cover. Microwave on high (100%) for about 7 minutes, stirring once at halftime, until chicken is no longer pink inside.

Stir sour cream into flour in small bowl until smooth. Add to chicken mixture. Stir. Cover. Microwave on medium (50%) for about 4 minutes until sauce is boiling and slightly thickened. Makes about 3 cups (750 mL). Toss with or spoon over noodles. Serves 4.

NUTRITION INFORMATION 1 serving: 443 Calories; 9.2 g Total Fat (4.3 g Mono, 1.6 g Poly, 4.2 g Sat); 75 mg Cholesterol; 53 g Carbohydrate; 4 g Fibre; 36 g Protein; 403 mg Sodium

CHOICES 3 Starch; 1/2 Fruit & Vegetable; 4 Protein

Turkey Roast Supreme

The tasty sauce keeps the turkey moist and delicious. Use leftovers in sandwiches or for lunch.

Whole baby carrots	**2 cups**	**500 mL**
Celery ribs, sliced	**3**	**3**
Olive (or canola) oil	**1 tbsp.**	**15 mL**
Sliced onion	**1 1/2 cups**	**375 mL**
Pepper	**1 tsp.**	**5 mL**
Garlic cloves, minced (or 1/2 tsp., 2 mL, powder)	**2**	**2**
Paprika	**1 tsp.**	**5 mL**
Olive (or canola) oil	**1 tsp.**	**5 mL**
Turkey breast roast	**2 1/2 lbs.**	**1.1 kg**
Low-sodium prepared chicken broth	**1 cup**	**250 mL**
Italian no-salt seasoning (such as Mrs. Dash), or mixture of dried rosemary, basil and parsley flakes	**2 tsp.**	**10 mL**
2% evaporated milk	**3/4 cup**	**175 mL**
All-purpose flour	**2 tbsp.**	**30 mL**

Layer carrots and celery in bottom of 3 1/2 quart (3.5 L) slow cooker.

Heat first amount of olive oil in large frying pan on medium. Add onion. Cook for about 10 minutes, stirring often, until onion is softened. Add to slow cooker.

Combine next 4 ingredients in small dish.

Rub into roast. Place roast on top of vegetables.

Pour broth around roast. Sprinkle with seasoning. Cover. Cook on Low for 7 to 8 hours or on High for 3 1/2 to 4 hours until desired doneness. Remove roast to plate. Tent with foil.

Stir evaporated milk into flour in small bowl until smooth. Add to slow cooker. Stir. Cover. Cook on High for about 15 minutes until boiling and slightly thickened. Makes 4 3/4 cups (1.2 L) vegetables and sauce. Thinly slice roast. Arrange on serving plate. Spoon vegetables and sauce over top. Serves 8 to 10.

NUTRITION INFORMATION 1 serving: 244 Calories; 3.5 g Total Fat (1.9 g Mono, 0.5 g Poly, 0.7 g Sat); 89 mg Cholesterol; 13 g Carbohydrate; 2 g Fibre; 39 g Protein; 215 mg Sodium

CHOICES 1 Fruit & Vegetable; 1/2 Milk; 5 Protein

Peanut Butter Chicken

A saucy chicken dish. Serve with rice, noodles or couscous.

Olive (or canola) oil	2 tsp.	10 mL
Medium onions, sliced	2	2
Garlic cloves, minced (or 1/2 tsp., 2 mL, powder)	2	2
Whole baby carrots	2 cups	500 mL
Bone-in chicken parts, skin removed	3 1/2 lbs.	1.6 kg
Can of tomato sauce	7 1/2 oz.	213 mL
Brown sugar, packed	1 tbsp.	15 mL
Curry powder	1 tsp.	5 mL
Peanut butter	1/2 cup	125 mL
Low-fat plain yogurt (not non-fat)	1/2 cup	125 mL
Olive (or canola) oil	2 tsp.	10 mL
Medium zucchini (with peel), quartered lengthwise and sliced crosswise into 3/4 inch (2 cm) pieces	2	2
Coarsely chopped roasted unsalted peanuts (optional)	2 tbsp.	30 mL

Heat first amount of olive oil in large non-stick frying pan on medium. Add onion and garlic. Cook for about 10 minutes, stirring often, until onion is softened and starting to brown. Transfer to 3 1/2 quart (3.5 L) slow cooker.

Layer carrots and chicken over onion mixture. Do not stir.

Combine tomato sauce, brown sugar and curry powder in small bowl. Spoon over chicken. Cover. Cook on Low for 7 to 8 hours or on High for 3 1/2 to 4 hours until chicken is no longer pink inside. Remove chicken to serving dish. Cover to keep warm.

Combine peanut butter and yogurt in small bowl. Add to slow cooker. Stir. Cover. Heat on Low for about 5 minutes until heated through.

Heat second amount of olive oil in large non-stick frying pan on medium-high. Add zucchini. Cook for about 5 minutes, stirring often, until slightly browned. Add to slow cooker. Stir. Pour sauce over chicken.

Sprinkle with peanuts. Makes 8 cups (2 L). Serves 8.

NUTRITION INFORMATION 1 serving: 304 Calories; 14.5 g Total Fat (6.8 g Mono, 3.4 g Poly, 3 g Sat); 68 mg Cholesterol; 18 g Carbohydrate; 4 g Fibre; 28 g Protein; 355 mg Sodium

CHOICES 1 1/2 Fruit & Vegetable; 4 Protein; 1/2 Fat & Oil

Pictured on page 72.

Slow Cooker Fajitas

Tender, spiced beef with both soft cooked and crisp, cold vegetables enclosed in a flour tortilla.

Beef sirloin tip steak, sliced into 3 inch (7.5 cm) thin strips	1 1/2 lbs.	680 g
Thickly sliced fresh white mushrooms	2 cups	500 mL
Red medium pepper, cut into 1/2 inch (12 mm) wide strips	1	1
Yellow medium pepper, cut into 1/2 inch (12 mm) wide strips	1	1
Large onion, cut lengthwise into 8 wedges	1	1
Finely chopped pickled jalapeño peppers, drained (optional)	1 tbsp.	15 mL
Package of fajita seasoning mix (use low-sodium if available)	1 oz.	28 g
Water	1/4 cup	60 mL
Medium flour tortillas (8 inch, 20 cm, diameter)	10	10
Medium avocado, peeled, pitted and diced	1	1
Lemon juice	2 tsp.	10 mL
Light (or fat-free) sour cream	2/3 cup	150 mL
Grated Monterey Jack With Jalapeño cheese	2/3 cup	150 mL
Medium tomato, seeded and diced	1	1
Shredded lettuce, packed	1 cup	250 mL

Place first 6 ingredients in 3 1/2 quart (3.5 L) slow cooker.

Combine seasoning mix and water in small dish. Add to slow cooker. Cover. Cook on Low for 5 to 6 hours or on High for 2 1/2 to 3 hours until beef is tender.

Strain beef and vegetables, reserving liquid for another purpose. Spoon about 1/2 cup (125 mL) beef mixture onto each tortilla.

Combine avocado and lemon juice in small bowl. Divide and spoon avocado mixture over beef mixture on each tortilla.

Divide sour cream, cheese, tomato and lettuce among fajitas. Fold bottom edge up and over filling. Fold in sides, leaving top open. Secure with wooden pick if desired. Makes 10 fajitas. Serves 6 to 8.

NUTRITION INFORMATION 1 serving: 495 Calories; 19.7 g Total Fat (9 g Mono, 2.9 g Poly, 8 g Sat); 71 mg Cholesterol; 46 g Carbohydrate; 5 g Fibre; 34 g Protein; 614 mg Sodium

CHOICES 2 Starch; 1 Fruit & Vegetable; 4 Protein; 1 1/2 Fat & Oil

Pictured on page 72.

Squash And Lentil Soup

A delicious, thick and hearty soup with a velvety smooth texture.

Canola oil	2 tsp.	10 mL
Chopped onion	2 cups	500 mL
Garlic cloves, minced (or 1/2 tsp., 2 mL, powder)	2	2
Finely grated, peeled gingerroot (or 1/4 tsp., 1 mL, ground ginger)	1 tsp.	5 mL
Curry powder	1 tbsp.	15 mL
Red lentils	1 1/2 cups	375 mL
Low-sodium prepared chicken broth	6 cups	1.5 L
Chopped butternut squash (about 1 1/2 lbs., 680 g)	5 cups	1.25 L
Salt	1/2 tsp.	2 mL
Low-fat plain yogurt	1/3 cup	75 mL

Heat canola oil in large frying pan on medium. Add onion, garlic and ginger. Cook for 5 to 10 minutes, stirring often, until onion is softened.

Add curry powder. Heat and stir for 1 to 2 minutes until fragrant. Transfer to 5 quart (5 L) slow cooker.

Add next 4 ingredients. Stir. Cover. Cook on Low for 6 to 8 hours or on High for 3 to 4 hours until lentils and squash are tender. Cool slightly. Process lentil mixture in blender or food processor until smooth. Return to slow cooker.

Add yogurt. Stir. Cover. Cook on High for about 15 minutes until heated through. Makes 9 1/2 cups (2.4 L). Serves 6 to 8.

NUTRITION INFORMATION 1 serving: 292 Calories; 2.7 g Total Fat (1.1 g Mono, 0.8 g Poly, 0.4 g Sat); 1 mg Cholesterol; 51 g Carbohydrate; 8 g Fibre; 20 g Protein; 858 mg Sodium

CHOICES 2 Starch; 1 1/2 Fruit & Vegetable; 2 Protein

To toast coconut, nuts and seeds, place in single layer in ungreased shallow pan. Bake in 350ºF (175ºC) oven for 5 to 10 minutes, stirring or shaking often, until desired doneness.

Orange Chicken

Tender chicken in an orange-flavoured sauce. Serve with rice and salad. This is a child-friendly entrée—no onions, no green bits and lots of those little orange pieces!

Hot water	1/4 cup	60 mL
Chicken bouillon powder (or low-sodium bouillon powder)	1 tsp.	5 mL
Can of unsweetened mandarin orange segments in juice	10 oz.	284 mL
Orange juice	1 cup	250 mL
Finely chopped fresh rosemary (or 1/2 tsp., 2 mL, dried)	2 tsp.	10 mL
Lemon pepper	1 tsp.	5 mL
Paprika	1/2 tsp.	2 mL
Salt (optional)	1/4 tsp.	1 mL
Bone-in chicken parts, skin removed	3 lbs.	1.4 kg
Water	2 tbsp.	30 mL
Cornstarch	2 tbsp.	30 mL

Stir hot water into bouillon powder in small bowl until dissolved.

Drain juice from oranges into same bowl. Set orange segments aside.

Add next 5 ingredients to juice mixture. Stir. Pour into 3 1/2 quart (3.5 L) slow cooker.

Add chicken, pressing meaty parts down into juice mixture. Cover. Cook on Low for 7 to 8 hours or on High for 3 1/2 to 4 hours until chicken is no longer pink inside.

Stir water into cornstarch in small bowl until smooth. Add to slow cooker. Stir. Cover. Cook on High for about 15 minutes until sauce is thickened. Add orange segments. Stir. Serves 4.

NUTRITION INFORMATION 1 serving: 267 Calories; 5.5 g Total Fat (1.6 g Mono, 1.3 g Poly, 1.4 g Sat); 115 mg Cholesterol; 17 g Carbohydrate; trace Fibre; 36 g Protein; 290 mg Sodium

CHOICES 1 1/2 Fruit & Vegetable; 5 Protein

Moroccan Chicken

Serve this spicy dish with couscous or Spinach Mushroom Rice, page 93. You'll enjoy this full-flavoured, well-seasoned sauce.

Canola oil	2 tsp.	10 mL
Thinly sliced onion	2 cups	500 mL
Garlic cloves, minced (or 1/2 tsp., 2 mL, powder)	2	2
Finely grated, peeled gingerroot	1/2 tsp.	2 mL
Ground cumin	1/2 tsp.	2 mL
Ground coriander	1/2 tsp.	2 mL
Chili powder	1/2 tsp.	2 mL
Boneless, skinless chicken thighs, halved	1 lb.	454 g
Salt, sprinkle		
Cinnamon stick (4 inch, 10 cm, length)	1	1
Cardamom pods, bruised (see Tip, page 23) or 1/4 tsp. (1 mL), ground	6	6
Dry white wine (or low-sodium prepared chicken broth)	1/2 cup	125 mL
Liquid honey	2 tbsp.	30 mL
Orange juice	1/4 cup	60 mL
Cornstarch	2 tsp.	10 mL
Slivered almonds, toasted (see Tip, page 63), optional	3 tbsp.	50 mL

Heat canola oil in large frying pan on medium. Add onion, garlic and ginger. Cook for 5 to 10 minutes, stirring often, until onion is softened and starting to brown.

Add cumin, coriander and chili powder. Heat and stir for 1 to 2 minutes until fragrant. Transfer to 5 quart (5 L) slow cooker.

Add next 6 ingredients. Stir. Cover. Cook on Low for 7 to 8 hours or on High for 3 1/2 to 4 hours until chicken is no longer pink inside.

Stir orange juice into cornstarch in small bowl until smooth. Stir into chicken mixture. Cover. Cook on High for about 15 minutes until thickened. Remove and discard cinnamon stick and cardamom pods.

Sprinkle with almonds. Makes 3 cups (750 mL). Serves 4.

NUTRITION INFORMATION 1 serving: 272 Calories; 8.8 g Total Fat (3.3 g Mono, 2.3 g Poly, 1.8 g Sat); 94 mg Cholesterol; 20 g Carbohydrate; 2 g Fibre; 23 g Protein; 9 mg Sodium

CHOICES 1 Fruit & Vegetable; 3 1/2 Protein; 1 Sugar

Pork With Orange Sauce

A tasty dish to serve a larger crowd or to enjoy as leftovers.

Apricot jam, warmed	1/4 cup	60 mL
Dijon mustard (with whole seeds)	2 tbsp.	30 mL
Salt, sprinkle		
Pepper, sprinkle		
Boneless pork sirloin end (or loin) roast	3 lbs.	1.4 kg
ORANGE SAUCE		
Hard margarine (or butter)	1 tsp.	5 mL
Finely chopped onion	1/4 cup	60 mL
Brandy (or 1 tsp., 5 mL, brandy flavouring)	3 tbsp.	50 mL
Orange juice	1 cup	250 mL
Low-sodium prepared chicken broth	1 cup	250 mL
Dijon mustard (with whole seeds)	1 tbsp.	15 mL
Water	1 tbsp.	15 mL
Cornstarch	2 tsp.	10 mL

Combine first 4 ingredients in small cup.

Brush apricot mixture over roast. Place roast in 5 quart (5 L) slow cooker. Cover. Cook on Low for about 8 hours until meat thermometer inserted into thickest part of roast reads 155°F (68°C), or until desired doneness. Remove roast. Cover with foil. Let stand for 10 minutes. Internal temperature should rise to at least 160°F (70°C).

Orange Sauce: Melt margarine in medium saucepan on medium. Add onion. Cook for 5 to 10 minutes, stirring often, until onion is softened and starting to brown. Add brandy. Heat and stir for about 2 minutes until brandy is almost evaporated.

Add orange juice, broth and mustard. Stir. Bring to a boil on medium-high. Boil, uncovered, for about 5 minutes until slightly reduced.

Stir water into cornstarch in small cup until smooth. Add to orange juice mixture. Heat and stir on medium for about 5 minutes until boiling gently and thickened. Makes 1 1/3 cups (325 mL) sauce. Cut roast into 1/3 inch (1 cm) thick slices. Serve with sauce. Serves 8.

NUTRITION INFORMATION 1 serving: 418 Calories; 24.2 g Total Fat (10.7 g Mono, 2.8 g Poly, 8.2 g Sat); 114 mg Cholesterol; 12 g Carbohydrate; trace Fibre; 34 g Protein; 261 mg Sodium

CHOICES 1 Fruit & Vegetable; 4 1/2 Protein; 2 Fat & Oil

Beef In Red Wine

A delicious and tender stew for very special occasions. Great served with mashed potatoes or noodles.

All-purpose flour	3 tbsp.	50 mL
Salt, sprinkle		
Beef stew meat, cubed	1 lb.	454 g
Canola oil	2 tsp.	10 mL
Thinly sliced onion	2 cups	500 mL
Thinly sliced carrot	1 cup	250 mL
Dry red (or alcohol-free) wine	1 cup	250 mL
Garlic cloves, minced (or 1/2 tsp., 2 mL, powder)	2	2
Sprig of fresh rosemary (or thyme)	1	1
Bay leaves	2	2
Pepper	1/4 tsp.	1 mL

Combine flour and salt in large plastic bag. Add beef. Shake until coated.

Heat canola oil in large frying pan on medium-high. Add beef. Cook for about 5 minutes, stirring occasionally, until browned. Transfer to 3 1/2 quart (3.5 L) slow cooker.

Add remaining 7 ingredients. Stir. Cover. Cook on Low for 6 to 8 hours or on High for 4 to 5 hours until beef is tender. Remove and discard rosemary sprig and bay leaves. Makes 3 cups (750 mL). Serves 4.

NUTRITION INFORMATION 1 serving: 444 Calories; 16.5 g Total Fat (7.4 g Mono, 1.6 g Poly, 5.6 g Sat); 84 mg Cholesterol; 24 g Carbohydrate; 4 g Fibre; 36 g Protein; 134 mg Sodium

CHOICES 1/2 Starch; 1 1/2 Fruit & Vegetable; 4 1/2 Protein; 1/2 Fat & Oil

Kid-Friendly Idea

Although the alcohol in the wine will evaporate during cooking, you may prefer to substitute the same amount of low-sodium beef broth.

NUTRITION INFORMATION 1/2 cup (125 mL): 333 Calories; 12.3 g Total Fat (5.6 g Mono, 1.2 g Poly, 4.2 g Sat); 63 mg Cholesterol; 18 g Carbohydrate; 3 g Fibre; 27 g Protein; 100 mg Sodium

CHOICES 1/2 Starch; 1 Fruit & Vegetable; 3 1/2 Protein; 1/2 Fat & Oil

Pineapple Chicken Skewers

Refreshing flavours of mint, lime and tomato with a colourful salsa.

LIME CHILI MARINADE

Lime juice	3 tbsp.	50 mL
Chili sauce	2 tbsp.	30 mL
Garlic clove, minced (or 1/4 tsp., 1 mL, powder)	1	1
Finely grated, peeled gingerroot	1 tsp.	5 mL
Sesame (or cooking) oil	1 tsp.	5 mL
Boneless, skinless chicken breast halves, cut into twenty-four, 3/4 inch (2 cm) cubes	1 lb.	454 g
Can of pineapple slices, drained, cut into 8 pieces each	14 oz.	398 mL
Bamboo skewers (8 inch, 20 cm, length), soaked in water for 10 minutes	8	8

TOMATO SALSA

Chopped seeded tomato	2/3 cup	150 mL
Chopped green onion	1/4 cup	60 mL
Chopped fresh mint leaves	1 tbsp.	15 mL
Lime juice	2 tsp.	10 mL
Sesame (or canola) oil	1/2 tsp.	2 mL
Finely grated lime zest	1/4 tsp.	1 mL
Pepper, sprinkle		

Lime Chili Marinade: Combine first 5 ingredients in medium bowl.

Add chicken. Stir. Let stand for 15 minutes.

Thread 8 pineapple pieces (2 together) and 3 chicken pieces alternately onto each skewer. Preheat greased two-sided grill for 5 minutes. Place skewers on grill. Close lid. Cook for about 5 minutes until chicken is no longer pink inside.

Tomato Salsa: Combine all 7 ingredients in small bowl. Makes about 3/4 cup (175 mL) salsa. Serve with skewers. Makes 8 skewers. Serves 4.

NUTRITION INFORMATION 1 serving: 285 Calories; 14.8 g Total Fat (5.5 g Mono, 5.8 g Poly, 2.4 g Sat); 66 mg Cholesterol; 12 g Carbohydrate; 2 Fibre; 26 g Protein; 120 mg Sodium

CHOICES 1 Fruit & Vegetable; 3 1/2 Protein; 1 Fat & Oil

Grilled Pork Mushrooms

Excellent served with Maple Butternut Squash, page 104, and a drizzle of Spicy Roasted Pepper Sauce, page 113.

Lean ground pork	**8 oz.**	**225 g**
Garlic clove, minced (or 1/4 – 1/2 tsp., 1 – 2 mL, powder)	**1 – 2**	**1 – 2**
Green onions, thinly sliced	**2**	**2**
Low-sodium soy sauce	**1 tbsp.**	**15 mL**
Finely chopped fresh parsley (or 3/4 tsp., 4 mL, flakes)	**1 tbsp.**	**15 mL**
Dry sherry	**2 tsp.**	**10 mL**
Egg white (large)	**1**	**1**
Dried crushed chilies	**1/4 tsp.**	**1 mL**
Pepper, sprinkle		
Portobello mushrooms (5 inch, 12.5 cm, diameter), stems removed	**4**	**4**
Sesame seeds	**1 tsp.**	**5 mL**
Paprika, sprinkle		

Put first 9 ingredients into medium bowl. Stir well. Makes 1 1/4 cups (300 mL) filling.

Scrape black "gills" with spoon from around underside of mushrooms and discard. Divide and spoon pork mixture into each cavity. Spread evenly.

Sprinkle with sesame seeds and paprika. Preheat greased two-sided grill for 5 minutes. Place mushrooms, stuffed side up, on grill. Close lid. Cook for about 5 minutes until pork is no longer pink. Makes 4 stuffed mushrooms. Serves 2.

NUTRITION INFORMATION 1 serving: 277 Calories; 8.6 g Total Fat (3.2 g Mono, 1.6 g Poly, 2.5 g Sat); 66 mg Cholesterol; 19 g Carbohydrate; 5 g Fibre; 34 g Protein; 355 mg Sodium

CHOICES 1 1/2 Fruit & Vegetable; 4 1/2 Protein

Apricot-Glazed Chicken

Moist chicken with a tangy glaze. Serve with Fluffy Garlic Potatoes, page 88, and Asparagus And Mushrooms, page 109.

APRICOT PURÉE

Can of apricots in light syrup, drained	**14 oz.**	**398 mL**
Brown sugar, packed	**1 tbsp.**	**15 mL**
Lemon juice	**2 tsp.**	**10 mL**
Garlic (or regular) chili sauce	**1 tsp.**	**5 mL**
Boneless, skinless chicken thighs (or breast halves)	**1 lb.**	**454 g**

Apricot Purée: Process first 4 ingredients in blender or food processor until smooth. Pour into large resealable freezer bag.

Add chicken. Seal bag. Turn until coated. Marinate in refrigerator for at least 24 hours, turning several times. Remove chicken from bag. Pour purée into small saucepan. Bring to a boil. Boil for about 5 minutes, stirring often, until reduced and slightly thickened. Preheat greased two-sided grill for 5 minutes. Place chicken on grill. Close lid. Cook for 5 to 7 minutes until no longer pink inside and browned outside. Remove to serving plate. Drizzle purée over chicken. Serves 4.

NUTRITION INFORMATION 1 serving: 183 Calories; 6.3 g Total Fat (2 g Mono, 1.6 g Poly, 1.6 g Sat); 94 mg Cholesterol; 9 g Carbohydrate; 1 g Fibre; 22 g Protein; 4 mg Sodium

CHOICES 1/2 Fruit & Vegetable; 3 Protein; 1/2 Sugar

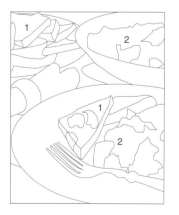

1. Mushroom Polenta, page 99
2. Chicken Cacciatore, page 48

Peppered Lamb

Tender lamb chops with a hint of garlic and mint flavour in the coating. These are so easy and flavourful that they will become a favourite. Serve with Creamed Veggie Spaghetti, page 94, and Zucchini Pepper Combo, page 105.

Finely chopped fresh mint (or 1 1/2 tsp., 7 mL, dried)	**2 tbsp.**	**30 mL**
Olive (or canola) oil	**1 tbsp.**	**15 mL**
Garlic cloves, minced (or 1/2 tsp., 2 mL, powder)	**2**	**2**
Pepper	**1/2 tsp.**	**2 mL**
Lean lamb chops (about 1 1/4 – 1 1/2 lbs., 560 – 680 g, total), about 1 1/4 inches (3 cm), thick (see Note)	**8**	**8**

Combine first 4 ingredients in small dish.

Spread mint mixture thinly onto both sides of each lamb chop. Let stand on plate at room temperature for 15 minutes. Preheat greased two-sided grill for 5 minutes. Place chops on grill. Close lid. Cook for 8 to 10 minutes until desired doneness. Remove to plate. Tent with foil. Let stand for 10 minutes before serving. Makes 8 lamb chops. Serves 4.

NUTRITION INFORMATION 1 serving: 157 Calories; 10.2 g Total Fat (5.2 g Mono, 0.9 g Poly, 1.4 g Sat); 48 mg Cholesterol; 1 g Carbohydrate; trace Fibre; 15 g Protein; 53 mg Sodium

CHOICES 2 Protein; 1 Fat

Pictured on page 36.

Note: Ask the butcher to chine or crack backbone to make serving easier.

1. Peanut Butter Chicken, page 61
2. Slow Cooker Fajitas, page 62

Orange Teriyaki Fish

Basa is a fleshy, moist white fish that absorbs marinade flavours easily. Serve with Mashed Sweet Potatoes, page 103.

Soy sauce (not low-sodium)	**2 tbsp.**	**30 mL**
Frozen concentrated orange juice, thawed	**2 tbsp.**	**30 mL**
Corn syrup	**1 tbsp.**	**15 mL**
Finely grated, peeled gingerroot	**1 tsp.**	**5 mL**
Lemon pepper	**1/2 tsp.**	**2 mL**
Frozen (or fresh) Basa (or other white fish) fillets, thawed (about 1 1/4 lbs., 560 g)	**4**	**4**

Combine first 5 ingredients in small cup.

Arrange fish, in single layer, in ungreased 9 x 13 inch (22 x 33 cm) pan. Spoon marinade over fish. Turn until coated. Cover. Marinate in refrigerator for 30 minutes. Preheat greased two-sided grill for 5 minutes. Place fish on grill. Close lid. Cook for about 4 minutes until fish flakes easily when tested with fork. Serves 4.

NUTRITION INFORMATION 1 serving: 195 Calories; 5.2 g Total Fat (2 g Mono, 1.5 g Poly, 1.1 g Sat); 95 mg Cholesterol; 8 g Carbohydrate; trace Fibre; 27 g Protein; 627 mg Sodium

CHOICES 1 Fruit & Vegetable; 4 Protein

Pesto Chicken Wraps

Attractive grilled tortillas are fully stuffed with fresh asparagus, peppers and chicken. Use a store-bought roasted chicken for this recipe to make it quicker and easier. Serve with a tomato and basil salad or Oven-Fried Vegetables, page 112.

Fresh asparagus (about 5 oz., 140 g), trimmed of tough ends	**6**	**6**
Boiling water		
Sun-dried tomato pesto	**1/3 cup**	**75 mL**
Ultra low-fat mayonnaise	**2 tbsp.**	**30 mL**
Large flour tortillas (10 inch, 25 cm, diameter)	**2**	**2**
Chopped cooked chicken (about 12 oz., 340 g)	**2 cups**	**500 mL**
Coarsely chopped roasted red peppers (see Note)	**1/2 cup**	**125 mL**
Thinly sliced fresh white mushrooms	**1/2 cup**	**125 mL**

Cook asparagus in small amount of boiling water in frying pan on medium-high for about 2 minutes until tender-crisp. Remove to paper towel to drain well.

(continued on next page)

Combine pesto and mayonnaise in small bowl. Spread onto 1 side of each tortilla.

Divide and place chicken, red pepper, asparagus and mushrooms down centre of each tortilla. Fold sides of tortilla over filling. Roll up from bottom to enclose filling. Preheat greased two-sided grill for 5 minutes. Place wraps on grill. Close lid. Cook for about 5 minutes until crisp and browned. To serve, cut each wrap in half diagonally. Serves 4.

NUTRITION INFORMATION 1 serving: 224 Calories; 4.8 g Total Fat (2.1 g Mono, 1.2 g Poly, 0.9 g Sat); 72 mg Cholesterol; 17 g Carbohydrate; 1 g Fibre; 28 g Protein; 180 mg Sodium

CHOICES 1 Starch; 4 Protein

Pictured on front cover.

Note: Roasted peppers are available in jars in most grocery stores. Drain well.

Mustard Dill Halibut

A sweet, tangy sauce coats these moist, tender fish steaks. Serve with Crunchy Rice Salad, page 96, and Pea Medley, page 110.

Maple (or maple-flavoured) syrup	**1/4 cup**	**60 mL**
Dijon mustard (with whole seeds)	**2 tbsp.**	**30 mL**
Chopped fresh dill (or 1 1/2 tsp., 7 mL, dill weed)	**2 tbsp.**	**30 mL**
Lemon juice	**2 tbsp.**	**30 mL**
Garlic clove, minced (or 1/4 tsp., 1 mL, powder)	**1**	**1**
Salt	**1/2 tsp.**	**2 mL**
Small halibut steaks (about 1 1/2 lbs., 680 g, total)	**4**	**4**

Combine first 6 ingredients in small bowl.

Place halibut in shallow dish. Pour maple syrup mixture over fish. Turn until coated. Marinate in refrigerator for 3 to 5 hours, turning several times. Drain and discard marinade. Preheat greased two-sided grill for 5 minutes. Place fish on grill. Close lid. Cook for 5 to 8 minutes until fish flakes easily when tested with fork. Serves 4.

NUTRITION INFORMATION 1 serving: 212 Calories; 4.1 g Total Fat (1.3 g Mono, 1.5 g Poly, 0.6 g Sat); 54 mg Cholesterol; 6 g Carbohydrate; trace Fibre; 36 g Protein; 243 mg Sodium

CHOICES 5 Protein; 1/2 Sugar

Pictured on page 36.

MUSTARD DILL SALMON: Omit halibut. Use same amount of salmon fillet or steak.

Grilled Chicken And Salsa

Lightly spiced chicken and bright, colourful salsa are a perfect match. Reserve some salsa for Beef And Rice Lettuce Wraps, page 77.

Lime juice	2 tbsp.	30 mL
Dried crushed chilies	1 tsp.	5 mL
Granulated sugar	1 tsp.	5 mL
Ground cinnamon	3/4 tsp.	4 mL
Ground cumin	1/2 tsp.	2 mL
Ground coriander	1/2 tsp.	2 mL
Garlic cloves, minced (or 1/2 tsp., 2 mL, powder)	2	2
Boneless, skinless chicken breast halves, flattened evenly	1 lb.	454 g
FRESH CORN SALSA		
Medium corncobs	2	2
Medium tomatoes, quartered, seeded and chopped	3	3
Can of black beans, rinsed and drained	19 oz.	540 mL
Finely chopped celery	1/2 cup	125 mL
Thinly sliced green onion	1/2 cup	125 mL
Lime juice	1/3 cup	75 mL
Chopped fresh parsley (or cilantro)	3 tbsp.	50 mL
Olive (or canola) oil	2 tsp.	10 mL
Ground cumin	1/4 tsp.	1 mL
Hot pepper sauce	1/4 tsp.	1 mL
Garlic clove, minced (or 1/4 tsp., 1 mL, powder)	1	1

Combine first 7 ingredients in large shallow dish.

Add chicken. Turn until coated. Cover. Marinate in refrigerator for at least 8 hours or overnight, turning several times.

Fresh Corn Salsa: Preheat electric grill for 5 minutes or gas barbecue to high. Cook corncobs on greased grill for about 15 minutes, turning often, until corn is tender and browned. Let stand until cool enough to handle. Place cob, 1 end down, on cutting board. Run knife down length of cob, cutting off kernels. Put kernels into medium bowl. Discard cob. Repeat with second cob. Add next 4 ingredients to corn. Stir.

Combine next 6 ingredients in jar with tight-fitting lid. Shake well. Drizzle over corn mixture. Toss well. Makes 5 1/2 cups (1.4 L) salsa. Reserve 3 1/2 cups (875 mL) salsa in airtight container in refrigerator to use for Beef And Rice Lettuce Wraps, page 77. Remove chicken. Discard marinade. Preheat electric grill for 5 minutes or gas barbecue to medium. Cook chicken on greased grill for about 5 minutes per side until no longer pink inside. Slice diagonally into 1/4 inch (6 mm) pieces. Serve remaining salsa with grilled chicken. Serves 4.

(continued on next page)

NUTRITION INFORMATION 1 serving: 208 Calories; 3.6 g Total Fat (1.2 g Mono, 0.8 g Poly, 0.7 g Sat); 66 mg Cholesterol; 16 g Carbohydrate; 3 g Fibre; 29 g Protein; 71 mg Sodium

CHOICES 1 Starch; 4 Protein

To Make Ahead: Marinate chicken and make salsa, omitting corn, the night before. Grill chicken and corn on electric grill or gas barbecue the next day. Add corn to salsa.

Kid-Friendly Idea

Omit dried crushed chilies and reduce strong spices by half.

Beef And Rice Lettuce Wraps

Moist beef, beans and rice fill large, fresh lettuce leaves. Fun to eat and mild-flavoured for kids.

Olive (or canola) oil	1 tsp.	5 mL
Extra lean ground beef	1/2 lb.	225 g
Chopped onion	1/2 cup	125 mL
Reserved Fresh Corn Salsa (from Grilled Chicken And Salsa, page 76), plus accumulated juice	3 1/2 cups	875 mL
Vegetable cocktail juice (such as V8)	1 cup	250 mL
Long grain white rice	2/3 cup	150 mL
Large lettuce leaves (butter, green leaf, red leaf or iceberg varieties), see Note	16 – 20	16 – 20

Heat olive oil in large saucepan on medium. Add beef and onion. Scramble-fry for about 5 minutes until beef is no longer pink and onion is softened.

Add salsa and cocktail juice. Bring to a boil. Add rice. Stir. Reduce heat to medium-low. Cover. Simmer for 15 to 20 minutes until rice is tender and liquid is absorbed. Remove from heat. Divide and spoon into 4 individual bowls.

To serve, spoon 3 to 4 tbsp. (50 to 60 mL) rice mixture into centre of each lettuce leaf. Fold sides in and bottom up to enclose. Serves 4.

NUTRITION INFORMATION 1 serving: 381 Calories; 8.8 g Total Fat (4.3 g Mono, 1 g Poly, 2.5 g Sat); 29 mg Cholesterol; 58 g Carbohydrate; 6 g Fibre; 20 g Protein; 505 mg Sodium

CHOICES 3 Starch; 1/2 Fruit & Vegetable; 2 Protein; 1/2 Fat & Oil

Note: Soft lettuce varieties like butter and leaf are much easier to fold around filling. Iceberg lettuce, however, gives a cool, crisp crunch in contrast to the warm, soft filling.

Grilled Pork Sandwich

A tasty pork sandwich that will become a favourite. Reserve half of marinade and two cutlets for Spinach And Pork Salad, page 79.

ZESTY MARINADE		
Lemon juice	1/2 cup	125 mL
Chopped fresh parsley (or 3 1/2 tsp., 17 mL, flakes)	1/3 cup	75 mL
Olive (or canola) oil	2 tbsp.	30 mL
Liquid honey	1 tbsp.	15 mL
Finely grated lemon zest	2 tsp.	10 mL
Chili paste (sambal oelek)	2 tsp.	10 mL
Garlic cloves, minced (or 1/2 tsp., 2 mL, powder)	2	2
Pepper	1/2 tsp.	2 mL
Lean pork cutlets (about 1 1/4 lbs., 560 g, total)	4	4
Sun-dried tomatoes in oil, drained and finely chopped	2 tbsp.	30 mL
Low-fat mayonnaise	2 tbsp.	30 mL
Crusty bread loaf (such as ciabatta), cut in half horizontally	1	1
Fresh spinach, stems removed, torn and lightly packed	1/2 cup	125 mL
Sliced fresh white mushrooms	1/2 cup	125 mL

Zesty Marinade: Combine first 8 ingredients in large bowl.

Add pork cutlets. Turn until coated. Cover. Marinate in refrigerator for at least 15 minutes. Preheat electric grill for 5 minutes or gas barbecue to medium. Cook 2 cutlets on greased grill for 3 to 4 minutes per side until tender. Reserve remaining 2 cutlets in marinade in refrigerator to use for Spinach And Pork Salad, page 79.

Combine sun-dried tomatoes and mayonnaise in small bowl.

Broil cut side of bread until lightly toasted. Spread mayonnaise mixture onto bottom half of bread loaf.

Layer cutlets, spinach and mushrooms over mayonnaise. Cover with top of bread loaf. Cut crosswise into 4 sandwiches.

NUTRITION INFORMATION 1 sandwich: 321 Calories; 10.1 g Total Fat (5.1 g Mono, 2.2 g Poly, 1.8 g Sat); 48 mg Cholesterol; 35 g Carbohydrate; trace Fibre; 22 g Protein; 419 mg Sodium

CHOICES 2 Starch; 1/2 Fruit & Vegetable; 2 1/2 Protein; 1/2 Fat & Oil

Pictured on page 107.

Spinach And Pork Salad

A large meal salad with a tart lemon flavour and a lingering chili heat.

Reserved Zesty Marinade and 2 cutlets (from Grilled Pork Sandwich, page 78)		
Fresh spinach, stems removed, lightly packed	**4 cups**	**1 L**
Can of chickpeas, rinsed and drained	**19 oz.**	**540 mL**
Fresh (or frozen) green beans, trimmed and blanched (see Note), about 1 1/2 cups (375 mL) uncut beans	**5 – 6 oz.**	**140 – 170 g**
Roma (plum) tomatoes, quartered lengthwise	**4**	**4**
Thinly sliced red onion	**1/2 cup**	**125 mL**
LEMON DRESSING		
Lemon juice	**1/4 cup**	**60 mL**
Chopped fresh parsley (or 1 1/2 tsp., 7 mL, dried)	**2 tbsp.**	**30 mL**
Olive (or canola) oil	**1 tbsp.**	**15 mL**
Chili paste (sambal oelek)	**1 tsp.**	**5 mL**
Salt, sprinkle		

Preheat electric grill for 5 minutes or gas barbecue to medium. Remove cutlets from marinade. Discard marinade. Cook cutlets on greased grill for 3 to 4 minutes per side until tender. Cut crosswise into thin strips.

Combine next 5 ingredients in large bowl. Add pork. Toss.

Lemon Dressing: Process all 5 ingredients in blender or food processor until smooth. Makes about 1/3 cup (75 mL) dressing. Drizzle over salad. Toss. Makes 12 cups (3 L) salad. Serves 4 to 6.

NUTRITION INFORMATION 1 serving: 313 Calories; 10.5 g Total Fat (5.8 g Mono, 1.7 g Poly, 1.9 g Sat); 48 mg Cholesterol; 33 g Carbohydrate; 7 g Fibre; 25 g Protein; 254 mg Sodium

CHOICES 1 Starch; 1 Fruit & Vegetable; 3 Protein; 1/2 Fat & Oil

Pictured on page 107.

Note: To blanch beans, add to boiling water in large saucepan. Cook for 3 minutes. Drain. Immediately plunge into ice water for about 10 minutes until cold. Drain well.

Kid-Friendly Idea

Substitute same amount of iceberg lettuce for the spinach. Reduce or omit chili paste.

Basic Beef Stew

Tender beef with honey and mint flavours, and a warm, pleasant spiciness. Serve with cooling plain yogurt and Easy Coucous, page 92. Reserve half of stew for Spicy Beef Pie, page 81.

Beef stew meat, trimmed of fat and cubed	**2 lbs.**	**900 g**
All-purpose flour	**1/4 cup**	**60 mL**
Canola oil	**2 tsp.**	**10 mL**
Canola oil	**2 tsp.**	**10 mL**
Chopped onion	**2 cups**	**500 mL**
Garlic cloves, minced (or 1/2 tsp., 2 mL, powder)	**2**	**2**
Ground cumin	**1 tsp.**	**5 mL**
Ground coriander	**1 tsp.**	**5 mL**
Ground ginger	**1 tsp.**	**5 mL**
Dried crushed chilies	**1 tsp.**	**5 mL**
Low-sodium prepared beef broth	**1 1/2 cups**	**375 mL**
Medium carrots, chopped	**2**	**2**
Chopped celery	**3/4 cup**	**175 mL**
Salt (optional)	**1/4 tsp.**	**1 mL**
Liquid honey	**1 tbsp.**	**15 mL**
Chopped fresh mint	**2 – 3 tbsp.**	**30 – 50 mL**

Combine beef and flour in plastic bag. Toss until coated. Shake excess flour from beef. Remove beef to plate. Heat first amount of canola oil in large non-stick frying pan on medium. Cook beef, in 2 batches, until browned. Transfer to large pot or Dutch oven. Cover to keep warm.

Heat second amount of canola oil in same pan on medium. Add onion and garlic. Cook for 5 to 10 minutes, stirring often, scraping up any browned bits from pan, until onion is softened.

Add next 4 ingredients. Heat and stir for 1 to 2 minutes until fragrant.

Add 1/2 cup (125 mL) broth to onion mixture. Stir. Add to beef. Add remaining broth, carrot, celery and salt. Bring to a boil on medium-high. Reduce heat to medium-low. Cover. Cook for about 1 1/2 hours until beef is tender. Simmer, uncovered, for 15 to 20 minutes until sauce is slightly thickened. Makes about 5 cups (1.25 L) stew. Reserve 1/2 of stew and store in airtight container in refrigerator to use for Spicy Beef Pie, page 81.

(continued on next page)

Add honey and mint to remaining stew. Heat and stir on medium until heated through. Makes 2 1/2 cups (625 mL). Serves 4.

NUTRITION INFORMATION 1 serving: 192 Calories; 6 g Total Fat (2.8 g Mono, 0.9 g Poly, 1.4 g Sat); 44 mg Cholesterol; 15 g Carbohydrate; 2 g Fibre; 20 g Protein; 259 mg Sodium

CHOICES 1 Fruit & Vegetable; 3 Protein; 1/2 Sugar

Pictured on page 90.

Kid-Friendly Idea

Reduce spices by half and omit crushed chilies.

Spicy Beef Pie

Satisfying and crispy pastry "puffs" cover richly flavoured and tender beef stew. So easy to make a completely different presentation of beef stew.

Reserved stew (from Basic Beef Stew, page 80)	**2 1/2 cups**	**625 mL**
Frozen phyllo pastry sheets, thawed according to package directions	**8**	**8**
Sesame seeds (optional)	**2 tsp.**	**10 mL**

Put stew into lightly greased 9 inch (22 cm) deep dish pie plate.

Spray 1 phyllo sheet with cooking spray. Bunch up loosely. Place on top of stew. Repeat with remaining phyllo sheets.

Lightly spray top of pie with cooking spray. Sprinkle with sesame seeds. Bake in 375°F (175ºC) oven for 20 to 25 minutes until beef mixture is hot and pastry is lightly browned. Serves 4.

NUTRITION INFORMATION 1 serving: 289 Calories; 8.4 g Total Fat (3.4 g Mono, 2.2 g Poly, 1.8 g Sat); 44 mg Cholesterol; 30 g Carbohydrate; 2 g Fibre; 22 g Protein; 474 mg Sodium

CHOICES 1 1/2 Starch; 1/2 Fruit & Vegetable; 3 Protein

Pictured on page 90.

Roasted Garlic Pork Supper

Pork is infused with a delicious roasted garlic flavour. Serve with unsweetened applesauce in place of traditional gravy. Reserve half of roast for Quick Pork With Noodles, page 83.

Pork sirloin end roast	2 1/4 lbs.	1 kg
Garlic cloves, halved lengthwise	6	6
Liquid honey	1 tbsp.	15 mL
Paprika	1 tsp.	5 mL
Dry mustard	1 tsp.	5 mL
Pepper	1 tsp.	5 mL
Whole baby carrots	2 cups	500 mL
Small onions (root ends left intact), quartered lengthwise into wedges	3	3
Red baby potatoes (with peel), halved	1 lb.	454 g
Pepper, sprinkle		
Chopped fresh parsley (optional)		

Cut 12 small Xs in top of roast. Insert 1/2 garlic clove into each X.

Combine next 4 ingredients in small dish. Spread over top of roast. Place in greased medium roaster.

Arrange carrots, onion and potato around roast. Sprinkle with second amount of pepper. Cover. Cook in 325°F (160°C) oven for 1 1/2 to 2 hours until carrots are tender and meat thermometer inserted into thickest part of roast reads 155°F (68°C) for medium or until desired doneness. Cover with foil. Let stand for 10 minutes. Internal temperature should rise to at least 160°F (70°C). Slice 1/2 of roast, reserving remaining roast for Quick Pork On Noodles, page 83. Arrange pork slices and vegetables on platter.

Sprinkle with parsley. Serves 4.

NUTRITION INFORMATION 1 serving: 359 Calories; 10.4 g Total Fat (4.7 g Mono, 0.9 g Poly, 3.7 g Sat); 67 mg Cholesterol; 38 g Carbohydrate; 5 g Fibre; 29 g Protein; 87 mg Sodium

CHOICES 1 Starch; 1 1/2 Fruit & Vegetable; 3 1/2 Protein

Kid-Friendly Idea

Omit garlic and reduce mustard.

Quick Pork With Noodles

Colourful medley of pasta and pork strips.

Hard margarine (or butter), softened	2 tsp.	10 mL
Finely chopped onion	1/2 cup	125 mL
Sliced fresh white mushrooms	1 1/2 cups	375 mL
Pepper	1/4 tsp.	1 mL
Green onions, thinly sliced	2	2
Finely chopped red pepper	1/4 cup	60 mL
Can of skim evaporated milk	13 1/2 oz.	385 mL
All-purpose flour	2 tbsp.	30 mL
Reserved pork (from Roasted Garlic Pork Supper, page 82), cut into thin strips	2 cups	500 mL
Light herb-flavoured spreadable cream cheese	3 tbsp.	50 mL
Chopped fresh parsley (or 1 1/2 tsp., 7 mL, flakes)	2 tbsp.	30 mL
Balsamic vinegar	1 tsp.	5 mL
Package of large yolk-free broad noodles	12 oz.	340 g
Boiling water	12 cups	3 L
Salt	1 tbsp.	15 mL

Finely chopped fresh parsley (optional)

Melt margarine in large non-stick frying pan on medium. Add onion, mushrooms and pepper. Cook for about 10 minutes, stirring often, until onion is softened and liquid is evaporated.

Add green onion and red pepper. Stir.

Stir evaporated milk into flour in small bowl until smooth. Stir into onion mixture. Cook and stir on medium until boiling and slightly thickened.

Add next 4 ingredients. Heat and stir until cheese is melted and pork is heated through. Keep warm.

Cook noodles in boiling water and salt in large uncovered pot or Dutch oven for about 10 minutes, stirring occasionally, until tender but firm. Drain. Return to pot. Add pork mixture. Toss until coated. Transfer to serving bowl. Makes 9 1/2 cups (2.4 L).

Garnish with parsley. Serves 6.

NUTRITION INFORMATION 1 serving: 456 Calories; 10.7 g Total Fat (4.6 g Mono, 1.1 g Poly, 3.7 g Sat); 52 mg Cholesterol; 58 g Carbohydrate; 2 g Fibre; 31 g Protein; 180 mg Sodium

CHOICES 3 Starch; 1/2 Fruit & Vegetable; 1 Milk; 3 Protein; 1/2 Fat & Oil

Creamy Chicken Spaghetti

Perfectly coated creamy pasta. Reserve half of sauce for Garden Chicken Stew, page 85.

CHICKEN SAUCE

Canola oil	2 tsp.	10 mL
Boneless, skinless chicken thighs, quartered	2 lbs.	900 g
Canola oil	2 tsp.	10 mL
Leeks (white and tender green parts), thinly sliced (about 1 cup, 250 mL)	2	2
Garlic cloves, minced (or 1 tsp., 5 mL, powder)	4	4
Sliced fresh white mushrooms	4 cups	1 L
All-purpose flour	1/4 cup	60 mL
Low-sodium prepared chicken broth	3 cups	750 mL
Dijon mustard (with whole seeds)	2 tbsp.	30 mL
Spaghetti	12 oz.	340 g
Boiling water	12 cups	3 L
Salt	1 tsp.	5 mL
Light sour cream	1/4 cup	60 mL
Chopped fresh basil (or 2 1/4 tsp., 11 mL, dried)	3 tbsp.	50 mL
Salt, sprinkle		
Pepper, sprinkle		

Chicken Sauce: Heat first amount of canola oil in large saucepan on medium-high. Cook chicken, in 2 to 3 batches, for about 3 minutes per side, stirring often, until lightly browned. Remove from saucepan. Cover to keep warm.

Heat second amount of canola oil in same saucepan on medium. Add leek, garlic and mushrooms. Cook for 5 to 10 minutes, stirring often, until leek is softened and mushrooms are browned.

Add flour. Heat and stir for 1 minute. Gradually stir in broth. Heat and stir on medium until boiling and thickened. Add mustard. Stir. Add chicken. Cook for about 15 minutes, stirring often, until chicken is tender. Makes 6 1/2 cups (1.6 L) sauce. Reserve 1/2 of sauce in airtight container in refrigerator to use for Garden Chicken Stew, page 85.

Cook spaghetti in boiling water and salt in large uncovered pot or Dutch oven for 10 to 12 minutes, stirring occasionally, until tender but firm. Drain. Return to same pot.

Add remaining 4 ingredients to remaining chicken mixture. Heat and stir on medium until heated through. Add to spaghetti. Toss until coated. Makes 7 cups (1.75 L). Serves 6.

(continued on next page)

NUTRITION INFORMATION 1 serving: 360 Calories; 7.6 g Total Fat (2.7 g Mono, 2.1 g Poly, 2.2 g Sat);
64 mg Cholesterol; 48 g Carbohydrate; 2 g Fibre; 24 g Protein; 206 mg Sodium

CHOICES 3 Starch; 2 1/2 Protein

Garden Chicken Stew

A hearty stew with a hint of lemon.

Reserved Chicken Sauce (from Creamy Chicken Spaghetti, page 84)	3 1/4 cups	800 mL
Medium potatoes, peeled and chopped	2	2
Medium carrots, chopped	2	2
Low-sodium prepared chicken broth	1/2 cup	125 mL
Garlic clove, minced (or 1/4 tsp., 1 mL, powder)	1	1
Frozen peas	2/3 cup	150 mL
Chopped fresh parsley, for garnish	3 tbsp.	50 mL
Finely grated lemon zest, for garnish	1 tsp.	5 mL

Combine first 5 ingredients in large pot or Dutch oven. Bring to a boil on medium-high. Reduce heat to medium-low. Cover. Cook for about 20 minutes, stirring occasionally, until vegetables are tender.

Add peas. Heat and stir for about 5 minutes until heated through. Remove from heat.

Sprinkle parsley and lemon zest over top. Stir. Makes 5 1/2 cups (1.4 L). Serves 4.

NUTRITION INFORMATION 1 serving: 349 Calories; 9.3 g Total Fat (3.3 g Mono, 2.6 g Poly, 1.9 g Sat);
93 mg Cholesterol; 38 g Carbohydrate; 5 g Fibre; 29 g Protein; 433 mg Sodium

CHOICES 1 1/2 Starch; 1 Fruit & Vegetable; 3 1/2 Protein

Kid-Friendly Idea

Omit garlic, parsley and lemon zest.

Penne And Meat Sauce

A thick, hearty, full-bodied meat sauce. The oregano, garlic and wine flavours are distinct and blend nicely. Reserve half of sauce for Potato Beef Pie, page 87.

GROUND BEEF SAUCE

Canola oil	2 tsp.	10 mL
Chopped onion	2 cups	500 mL
Garlic cloves, minced (or 1/2 tsp., 2 mL, powder)	2	2
Extra lean ground beef	2 lbs.	900 g
Can of diced tomatoes (with juice)	28 oz.	796 mL
Red (or alcohol-free) wine	1 cup	250 mL
Can of tomato paste	5 1/2 oz.	156 mL
Chopped fresh oregano (or 1 1/2 tsp., 7 mL, dried)	2 tbsp.	30 mL
Granulated sugar	1 tsp.	5 mL
Bay leaf	1	1
Salt, sprinkle		
Pepper	1/4 tsp.	1 mL
Penne pasta (about 12 oz., 340 g)	3 cups	750 mL
Boiling water	12 cups	3 L
Salt	1 tsp.	5 mL
Finely grated fresh Parmesan cheese, sprinkle (optional)		

Ground Beef Sauce: Heat canola oil in large pot or Dutch oven on medium. Add onion and garlic. Cook for 5 to 10 minutes, stirring often, until onion is softened.

Add ground beef. Scramble-fry on medium-high for about 15 minutes until no pink remains.

Add next 8 ingredients. Stir. Bring to a boil. Reduce heat to medium-low. Cook, uncovered, for about 20 minutes, stirring occasionally, until sauce is thickened. Makes 7 cups (1.75 L) sauce. Reserve 1/2 of sauce in airtight container in refrigerator to use for Potato Beef Pie, page 87.

Cook pasta in boiling water and salt in large uncovered pot or Dutch oven for 10 to 12 minutes, stirring occasionally, until tender but firm. Drain. Turn pasta into large serving bowl or individual bowls. Spoon remaining sauce over top.

Sprinkle with Parmesan cheese. Serves 4.

NUTRITION INFORMATION 1 serving: 577 Calories; 12.3 g Total Fat (5 g Mono, 1.5 g Poly, 4 g Sat); 58 mg Cholesterol; 77 g Carbohydrate; 5 g Fibre; 33 g Protein; 230 mg Sodium

CHOICES 4 Starch; 1 Fruit & Vegetable; 3 1/2 Protein; 1/2 Fat & Oil

Potato Beef Pie

Great meal for everyone—warm and inviting.

MASHED POTATO TOPPING		
Medium potatoes (about 4), peeled and chopped	2 lbs.	900 g
Boiling water		
Salt	1/2 tsp.	2 mL
Milk	1 – 2 tbsp.	15 – 30 mL
Pepper	1/8 tsp.	0.5 mL
BEEF FILLING		
Reserved Ground Beef Sauce (from Penne And Meat Sauce, page 86)	3 1/2 cups	875 mL
Frozen mixed vegetables, thawed	1 1/2 cups	375 mL
Ketchup	3 tbsp.	50 mL
Worcestershire sauce	2 tsp.	10 mL
Finely grated fresh Parmesan cheese	1/4 cup	60 mL
Chopped fresh parsley, for garnish	1 tbsp.	15 mL

Mashed Potato Topping: Cook potato in boiling water and salt in medium saucepan on medium for about 15 minutes until tender. Drain. Mash potato until no lumps remain.

Add milk and pepper. Mix well. Makes 3 1/3 cups (825 mL) topping.

Beef Filling: Combine first 4 ingredients in medium bowl. Transfer to greased 2 quart (2 L) casserole. Smooth top. Spread potato topping evenly over top.

Sprinkle with Parmesan cheese. Bake in 400°F (205°C) oven for about 30 minutes until heated through.

Sprinkle with parsley. Let stand for 10 minutes before serving. Serves 4.

NUTRITION INFORMATION 1 serving: 531 Calories; 13.7 g Total Fat (5.5 g Mono, 1.2 g Poly, 5.3 g Sat); 63 mg Cholesterol; 68 g Carbohydrate; 8 g Fibre; 33 g Protein; 564 mg Sodium

CHOICES 2 Starch; 3 Fruit & Vegetable; 3 1/2 Protein; 1/2 Fat & Oil

Fluffy Garlic Potatoes

Fluffy mashed potatoes with lots of fresh parsley flecks and a tangy garlic flavour. A wonderful addition to any grilled or roasted entrée.

Medium baking potatoes, peeled and quartered	4	4
Water		
Salt	1/4 tsp.	1 mL
Low-fat plain yogurt	3 tbsp.	50 mL
Chopped fresh parsley (or 1 1/2 tsp., 7 mL, flakes)	2 tbsp.	30 mL
Garlic clove, minced (or 1/4 tsp., 1 mL, powder)	1	1
Pepper	1/4 tsp.	1 mL

Cook potato in water and salt in medium saucepan on medium-high for about 20 minutes until tender. Drain. Mash well.

Add remaining 4 ingredients. Stir with fork to make fluffy and remove lumps. Makes 2 1/2 cups (625 mL).

NUTRITION INFORMATION 1/2 cup (125 mL): 115 Calories; 0.3 g Total Fat (0.1 g Mono, 0.1 g Poly, 0.1 g Sat); 1 mg Cholesterol; 25 g Carbohydrate; 2 g Fibre; 3 g Protein; 16 mg Sodium

CHOICES 1 1/2 Starch

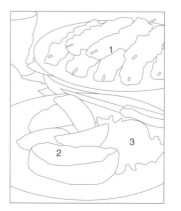

1. Pepper Pork Skewers, page 38
2. Crispy Spiced Potatoes, page 100
3. Lemon Garlic Steaks, page 16

Warm Potato Salad

This tangy, creamy dressing enhances the fresh, sweet taste of baby potatoes. Full flavour in a low-fat recipe!

Red baby potatoes (with peel), halved	**2 lbs.**	**900 g**
Salt, sprinkle		
Pepper	**1/4 tsp.**	**1 mL**
Finely chopped red onion	**1/3 cup**	**75 mL**
Ultra low-fat mayonnaise (not salad dressing)	**1/4 cup**	**60 mL**
Finely chopped gherkins (or dill pickles)	**1/4 cup**	**60 mL**
Fat-free sour cream	**2 – 3 tbsp.**	**30 – 50 mL**
Chopped fresh dill (or 1/2 tsp., 2 mL, dill weed)	**2 tsp.**	**10 mL**

Arrange potatoes, cut-side up, in single layer on greased baking sheet. Spray with cooking spray. Sprinkle with salt and pepper. Bake in 400°F (205°C) oven for about 45 minutes until crisp and golden.

Combine remaining 5 ingredients in large bowl. Add potatoes. Toss until coated. Makes 4 cups (1 L).

NUTRITION INFORMATION 1/2 cup (125 mL): 104 Calories; 0.2 g Total Fat (0 g Mono, 0.1 g Poly, 0 g Sat); 0 mg Cholesterol; 24 g Carbohydrate; 2 g Fibre; 3 g Protein; 159 mg Sodium

CHOICES 1 1/2 Starch

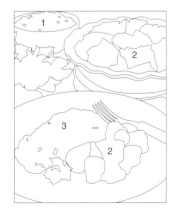

1. Spicy Beef Pie, page 81
2. Basic Beef Stew, page 80
3. Easy Couscous, page 92

Easy Couscous

Fluffy, golden couscous speckled with green onion and fresh parsley. Subtle cumin and ginger spices add an exotic flavour. Makes a delicious side dish for Spice Blackened Snapper, page 27, or Marinated Halibut Skewers, page 31.

Olive (or canola) oil	1 tsp.	5 mL
Chopped green onion	1 cup	250 mL
Ground cumin	1/2 tsp.	2 mL
Ground ginger	1/2 tsp.	2 mL
Garlic clove, minced (or 1/4 tsp., 1 mL, powder)	1	1
Liquid honey	1 tbsp.	15 mL
Low-sodium prepared chicken broth	2 cups	500 mL
Whole wheat (or plain) couscous	2 cups	500 mL
Olive (or canola) oil	2 tsp.	10 mL
Chopped fresh parsley (or 2 1/4 tsp., 11 mL, flakes)	3 tbsp.	50 mL
Salt, sprinkle (optional)		
Pepper, sprinkle		

Heat first amount of olive oil in medium saucepan on medium. Add next 4 ingredients. Cook and stir for about 3 minutes until green onion is softened.

Add honey. Heat and stir for about 30 seconds until green onion is coated.

Add broth. Bring to a boil. Add couscous and second amount of olive oil. Stir. Cover. Remove from heat. Let stand for 5 minutes without lifting lid. Fluff with fork.

Stir in remaining 3 ingredients. Makes 5 1/2 cups (1.4 L).

NUTRITION INFORMATION 1/2 cup (125 mL): 157 Calories; 1.5 g Total Fat (1 g Mono, 0.2 g Poly, 0.2 g Sat); 0 mg Cholesterol; 30 g Carbohydrate; 2 g Fibre; 5 g Protein; 122 mg Sodium

CHOICES 2 Starch; 1/2 Fat & Oil

Pictured on page 90.

Kid-Friendly Idea

Omit green onion, cumin and ginger.

Spinach Mushroom Rice

The wonderful aroma of jasmine rice is a perfect complement to the spinach and mushroom flavour. Serve with Succulent Lamb Chops, page 37, or Moroccan Chicken, page 65.

Jasmine rice (or 3/4 cup, 175 mL, long grain white rice)	1 cup	250 mL
Water	1 1/2 cups	375 mL
Salt (optional)	1/4 tsp.	1 mL
Canola oil	2 tsp.	10 mL
Finely chopped onion	1 cup	250 mL
Garlic clove, minced (or 1/4 tsp., 1 mL, powder)	1	1
Sliced fresh white mushrooms	3 cups	750 mL
Low-sodium prepared chicken broth	1/2 cup	125 mL
Chopped fresh spinach, stems removed	3 cups	750 mL
Light sour cream	3 tbsp.	50 mL

Combine rice, water and salt in medium saucepan. Bring to a boil. Reduce heat to low. Cover. Cook for 15 minutes. Remove from heat. Let stand for 5 minutes without lifting lid. Fluff with fork. Cover to keep warm.

Heat canola oil in large non-stick frying pan on medium. Add onion and garlic. Cook for about 5 minutes, stirring often, until onion is softened.

Add mushrooms. Cook for 7 to 10 minutes, stirring occasionally, until mushrooms are lightly browned and liquid is evaporated.

Add broth. Bring to a boil. Add spinach. Heat and stir for about 1 minute until spinach is just wilted. Remove from heat.

Stir in sour cream. Add rice. Stir. Makes 4 1/2 cups (1.1 L).

NUTRITION INFORMATION 1/2 cup (125 mL): 112 Calories; 1.7 g Total Fat (0.9 g Mono, 0.5 g Poly, 0.6 g Sat); 1 mg Cholesterol; 21 g Carbohydrate; 1 g Fibre; 3 g Protein; 56 mg Sodium

CHOICES 1 Starch; 1/2 Fruit & Vegetable;1/2 Fat & Oil

Pictured on page 53.

Kid-Friendly Idea

Chop spinach and mushrooms quite fine so there are no large pieces.

Creamed Veggie Spaghetti

Lots of colourful vegetables in a creamy, basil-flavoured sauce. Make this dish as spicy as you like by adjusting the fresh chilies, but note it is very spicy as is. Makes a great vegetarian entrée or a side dish for grilled fish or meat.

Whole wheat spaghetti	8 oz.	225 g
Boiling water	8 cups	2 L
Fresh asparagus, trimmed of tough ends, cut into 2 inch (5 cm) pieces	1 lb.	454 g
Olive (or canola) oil	1 tbsp.	15 mL
Garlic cloves, minced (or 1/2 tsp., 2 mL, powder), optional	2	2
Slivered red pepper	1 1/2 cups	375 mL
Sliced fresh brown (or white) mushrooms	1 1/2 cups	375 mL
Finely diced fresh red or green chilies, seeds removed (optional), see Tip, page 113	1 tbsp.	15 mL
Can of skim evaporated milk	13 1/2 oz.	385 mL
Skim milk	1/2 cup	125 mL
Cornstarch	2 tbsp.	30 mL
Finely grated fresh Romano (or Parmesan) cheese	1/3 cup	75 mL
Finely chopped fresh basil (or 1 1/4 tsp., 6 mL, dried)	1 1/2 tbsp.	25 mL
Pepper	1/2 tsp.	2 mL

Cook spaghetti in boiling water in large uncovered pot or Dutch oven for 6 minutes until partially cooked. Add asparagus. Stir. Boil for 3 to 4 minutes until spaghetti is tender but firm. Drain. Rinse with cold water. Drain well. Transfer to large serving bowl. Cover to keep warm.

Heat olive oil in same large pot on medium. Add next 4 ingredients. Cook for about 5 minutes, stirring often, until vegetables are slightly softened. Add to spaghetti. Cover to keep warm.

Heat evaporated milk in same pot on medium until hot.

Stir skim milk into cornstarch in small cup until smooth. Stir into evaporated milk. Heat and stir until boiling and thickened. Remove from heat.

Add Romano cheese, basil and pepper. Stir until cheese is melted. Add to spaghetti mixture. Toss until coated. Serve immediately. Makes 8 cups (2 L).

(continued on next page)

NUTRITION INFORMATION 1 cup (250 mL): 201 Calories; 3.2 g Total Fat (1.6 g Mono, 0.4 g Poly, 0.9 g Sat); 5 mg Cholesterol; 35 g Carbohydrate; 4 g Fibre; 11 g Protein; 104 mg Sodium

CHOICES 1 Starch ; 1 Fruit & Vegetable; 1 Milk; 1/2 Protein; 1/2 Fat & Oil

Pictured on page 108.

Kid-Friendly Idea

Omit fresh chilies and reduce or eliminate red pepper.

Tomato Herb Pasta

Rich flavour in a light tomato and herb sauce. Even better with a sprinkle of fresh Parmesan or ricotta cheese.

Penne pasta (about 12 oz., 340 g)	3 cups	750 mL
Boiling water	9 cups	2.25 L
Salt	1/4 tsp.	1 mL
Olive (or canola) oil	2 tsp.	10 mL
Finely chopped red onion	1 cup	250 mL
Garlic clove, minced (or 1/4 tsp., 1 mL, powder)	1	1
Medium roma (plum) tomatoes, chopped	6	6
Chopped fresh basil (or 1 1/2 tsp., 7 mL, dried)	2 tbsp.	30 mL
Chopped fresh parsley (or 1 1/2 tsp., 7 mL, flakes)	2 tbsp.	30 mL
Sweet (or regular) chili sauce	1 – 2 tbsp.	15 – 30 mL

Cook pasta in boiling water and salt in large uncovered pot or Dutch oven for 12 to 15 minutes, stirring occasionally, until tender but firm. Drain well. Return to pot. Cover to keep warm.

Heat olive oil in large frying pan on medium. Add onion and garlic. Cook for 5 to 10 minutes, stirring often, until onion is softened.

Add remaining 4 ingredients. Heat and stir for about 5 minutes until tomatoes are wilted. Add to pasta. Toss. Makes 5 cups (1.25 L).

NUTRITION INFORMATION 1 cup (250 mL): 288 Calories; 3.4 g Total Fat (1.6 g Mono, 0.8 g Poly, 0.5 g Sat); 0 mg Cholesterol; 56 g Carbohydrate; 4 g Fibre; 10 g Protein; 66 mg Sodium

CHOICES 3 Starch; 1/2 Fruit & Vegetable; 1/2 Protein; 1/2 Fat & Oil

Creamy Corn And Onion

Caramelized onion and parsley add extra flavour to sweet corn.

Canola oil	2 tsp.	10 mL
Thinly sliced onion	1 cup	250 mL
All-purpose flour	2 tsp.	10 mL
Brown sugar, packed	1 tsp.	5 mL
Balsamic vinegar	1 tsp.	5 mL
Salt, sprinkle		
Milk	3/4 cup	175 mL
Pepper	1/4 tsp.	1 mL
Can of kernel corn, drained	12 oz.	341 mL
Chopped fresh parsley (or 2 1/4 tsp., 11 mL, flakes)	3 tbsp.	50 mL

Heat canola oil in large frying pan on medium. Add onion. Cook for about 10 minutes, stirring often, until onion is soft and golden.

Add next 4 ingredients. Heat and stir for 1 minute.

Stir in milk. Add pepper. Heat and stir for about 2 minutes until boiling and thickened.

Add corn and parsley. Heat and stir until corn is heated through. Makes about 2 cups (500 mL).

NUTRITION INFORMATION 1/2 cup (125 mL): 127 Calories; 3.3 g Total Fat (1.6 g Mono, 0.9 g Poly, 0.6 g Sat); 2 mg Cholesterol; 23 g Carbohydrate; 2 g Fibre; 4 g Protein; 233 mg Sodium

CHOICES 1 1/2 Fruit & Vegetable; 1 Milk; 1/2 Fat & Oil

Crunchy Rice Salad

Bright, crispy vegetables with rice and pineapple. Coconut gives the salad unique flavour.

Cold cooked jasmine (or other) rice (2/3 cup, 150 mL, uncooked)	2 cups	500 mL
Can of pineapple tidbits, drained	14 oz.	398 mL
Can of water chestnuts, drained and chopped	8 oz.	227 mL
Diced celery	1/2 cup	125 mL
Diced red pepper	1/2 cup	125 mL
Diced red onion	1/2 cup	125 mL

(continued on next page)

LIME DRESSING

Lime juice	3 tbsp.	50 mL
Canola oil	1 tbsp.	15 mL
Low-sodium soy sauce	1 tbsp.	15 mL
Sweet (or regular) chili sauce	1 tbsp.	15 mL
Long thread (or flake) coconut, toasted (see Tip, page 63), for garnish	1/4 cup	60 mL

Toss first 6 ingredients in large bowl.

Lime Dressing: Combine first 4 ingredients in jar with tight-fitting lid. Shake well. Makes 1/3 cup (75 mL) dressing. Drizzle over rice mixture. Toss. Sprinkle with coconut. Makes 5 cups (1.25 L).

NUTRITION INFORMATION 1/2 cup (125 mL): 118 Calories; 3.1 g Total Fat (0.9 g Mono, 0.5 g Poly, 1.5 g Sat); 0 mg Cholesterol; 21 g Carbohydrate; 1 g Fibre; 2 g Protein; 81 mg Sodium

CHOICES 1 Starch; 1/2 Fruit & Vegetable; 1/2 Fat & Oil

Pictured on page 108.

Pasta Salad

A great balance of flavours that taste like summer.

LEMON DRESSING

Low-fat mayonnaise	1/3 cup	75 mL
Chopped fresh parsley (or 2 1/4 tsp., 11 mL, flakes)	3 tbsp.	50 mL
Lemon juice	1 – 2 tbsp.	15 – 30 mL
Liquid honey	1 tbsp.	15 mL
Garlic clove, minced (or 1/4 tsp., 1 mL, powder)	1	1
Pepper	1/4 tsp.	1 mL
Cooked penne pasta (about 8 oz., 250 g, dried)	2 cups	500 mL
Medium tomatoes, seeded and chopped	2	2
Chopped green onion	1/2 cup	125 mL
Can of artichoke hearts, drained and chopped	14 oz.	398 mL

Lemon Dressing: Combine first 6 ingredients in large bowl. Makes 1/2 cup (125 mL) dressing.

Add remaining 4 ingredients. Toss until coated. Makes 6 cups (1.5 L).

NUTRITION INFORMATION 1/2 cup (125 mL): 119 Calories; 2.2 g Total Fat (1.1 g Mono, 0.7 g Poly, 0.2 g Sat); 0 mg Cholesterol; 22 g Carbohydrate; 2 g Fibre; 4 g Protein; 116 mg Sodium

CHOICES 1 Starch; 1/2 Fruit & Vegetable; 1/2 Fat & Oil

Fried Rice

Very colourful with peas, green onion and red peppers. Earthy Chinese mushroom flavour with a nice crunch from fresh bean sprouts.

Chinese dried mushrooms	**6**	**6**
Boiling water	**2 cups**	**500 mL**
Canola oil	**2 tsp.**	**10 mL**
Chopped green onion	**1/3 cup**	**75 mL**
Finely chopped red pepper	**1/2 cup**	**125 mL**
Cooked long grain white rice (1 cup, 250 mL, uncooked)	**3 cups**	**750 mL**
Frozen peas	**1/2 cup**	**125 mL**
Finely chopped fat-free cooked ham (optional)	**1/3 cup**	**75 mL**
Low-sodium soy sauce	**2 tbsp.**	**30 mL**
Chili powder	**1/2 tsp.**	**2 mL**
Fresh bean sprouts, trimmed	**1 1/2 cups**	**375 mL**

Place mushrooms in small bowl. Cover with boiling water. Let stand for about 20 minutes until softened. Drain. Remove and discard stems. Finely chop caps.

Heat wok or large frying pan on medium until hot. Add canola oil. Add green onion and red pepper. Stir-fry for about 1 minute until onion is softened.

Add mushrooms. Add next 5 ingredients. Stir-fry for about 5 minutes until hot.

Add bean sprouts. Stir-fry about 1 minute until heated through. Makes 6 cups (1.5 L).

NUTRITION INFORMATION 1 cup (250 mL): 192 Calories; 2.1 g Total Fat (1.0 g Mono, 0.6 g Poly, 0.2 g Sat); 0 mg Cholesterol; 38 g Carbohydrate; 2 g Fibre; 5 g Protein; 184 mg Sodium

CHOICES 2 Starch; 1/2 Fruit & Vegetable; 1/2 Fat & Oil

Pictured on page 17.

Kid-Friendly Idea

Omit the mushrooms and bean sprouts.

NUTRITION INFORMATION 1 cup (250 mL): 173 Calories; 2 g Total Fat (1 g Mono, 0.6 g Poly, 0.2 g Sat); 0 mg Cholesterol; 34 g Carbohydrate; 1 g Fibre; 4 g Protein; 182 mg Sodium

CHOICES 2 Starch; 1/2 Fruit & Vegetable; 1/2 Fat & Oil

Mushroom Polenta

Peppery mushroom flavours in a thick, creamy textured polenta. An attractive alternative to pasta or potato.

Canola oil	2 tsp.	10 mL
Sliced fresh white mushrooms	2 cups	500 mL
Salt, sprinkle		
Low-sodium prepared chicken (or vegetable) broth	4 cups	1 L
Yellow cornmeal (polenta or corn grits)	1 1/2 cups	375 mL
Grated low-fat medium Cheddar cheese	1/2 cup	125 mL
Chopped fresh chives (or 2 1/2 tsp., 12 mL, dried)	3 tbsp.	50 mL
Pepper	1/4 tsp.	1 mL

Heat canola oil in large saucepan on medium-high. Add mushrooms and salt. Heat and stir for about 5 minutes until mushrooms are softened and beginning to brown. Transfer to small bowl.

Heat broth in same saucepan until boiling. Reduce heat to medium-low. Add cornmeal in slow, steady stream, stirring constantly. Heat and stir for about 10 minutes until soft and thick.

Add mushrooms. Add remaining 3 ingredients. Stir. Spread cornmeal mixture in greased 9 x 13 inch (22 x 33 cm) pan. Smooth top. Cool for 30 minutes. Cover. Chill for 1 to 2 hours until set. Cut into 12 equal pieces. Spray both sides of polenta pieces with cooking spray. Cook in large greased frying pan or on greased electric grill or gas barbecue on medium for about 3 minutes per side until lightly golden. Makes 12 pieces.

NUTRITION INFORMATION 1 piece: 100 Calories; 2.3 g Total Fat (0.9 g Mono, 0.4 g Poly, 0.8 g Sat); 4 mg Cholesterol; 15 g Carbohydrate; 1 g Fibre; 4 g Protein; 251 mg Sodium

CHOICES 1 Starch; 1/2 Protein

Pictured on page 71.

Crispy Spiced Potatoes

Flavourful herb and spice-speckled potato wedges. Outside edges are crispy and inside is soft and moist.

Egg whites (large), room temperature	2	2
Large red potatoes (with peel)	4	4
Chopped fresh rosemary (not dried)	2 tsp.	10 mL
Lemon pepper	1 tsp.	5 mL
Ground cumin	1/2 tsp.	2 mL
Garlic powder	1/2 tsp.	2 mL

Beat egg whites in extra-large bowl until just frothy. Do not overbeat.

Cut potatoes lengthwise in half. Cut each half lengthwise into 4 wedges. Add to egg whites. Toss until coated. Arrange in single layer on greased baking sheet.

Combine remaining 4 ingredients in small bowl. Sprinkle over potato wedges. Bake in 400°F (205°C) oven for about 1 hour, turning after 30 minutes, until crisp and golden. Makes 32 wedges.

NUTRITION INFORMATION 4 wedges: 122 Calories; 0.2 g Total Fat (0 g Mono, 0.1 g Poly, 0 g Sat); 0 mg Cholesterol; 26 g Carbohydrate; 3 g Fibre; 4 g Protein; 25 mg Sodium

CHOICES 1 1/2 Starch

Pictured on page 89.

Kid-Friendly Idea

Take away their forks and add a small bowl of light sour cream or ketchup for dipping. Kids will usually eat potatoes this way.

Potato Salad

A wonderful mix of red potatoes and crisp radishes in a creamy yogurt dressing. The goat cheese adds a zesty burst of flavour.

Baby red potatoes (with peel), halved	**2 lbs.**	**900 g**
Water		
Ice water		
Thinly sliced radishes	**3/4 cup**	**175 mL**
Alfalfa sprouts	**2/3 cup**	**150 mL**
Soft goat (chevré) cheese (about 3 oz., 85 g)	**1/3 cup**	**75 mL**
YOGURT AND HERB DRESSING		
Low-fat plain yogurt	**1/2 cup**	**125 mL**
Low-fat French dressing	**2 tbsp.**	**30 mL**
Chopped fresh mint leaves (or 1 1/2 tsp., 7 mL, dried)	**2 tbsp.**	**30 mL**
Chopped fresh chives (or 1 1/2 tsp., 7 mL, dried)	**2 tbsp.**	**30 mL**

Cook potato in water in large pot or Dutch oven on medium for about 15 minutes until just tender. Drain.

Immediately plunge potato into large bowl of ice water. Let stand for about 5 minutes until cool. Drain well. Remove to paper towels to dry completely. Transfer to separate large bowl.

Add radishes, alfalfa sprouts and cheese. Stir.

Yogurt And Herb Dressing: Combine all 4 ingredients in jar with tight-fitting lid. Shake well. Makes 2/3 cup (150 mL) dressing. Drizzle over potato mixture. Toss. Makes 6 cups (1.5 L).

NUTRITION INFORMATION 1 cup (250 mL): 175 Calories; 4.2 g Total Fat (1.1 g Mono, 0.4 g Poly, 2.4 g Sat); 8 mg Cholesterol; 28 g Carbohydrate; 4 g Fibre; 7 g Protein; 189 mg Sodium

CHOICES 1 1/2 Starch; 1/2 Protein; 1/2 Fat & Oil

Pictured on page 108.

Kid-Friendly Idea

Omit the radishes, alfalfa sprouts and goat cheese. Add 1/2 cup (125 mL) grated light sharp Cheddar cheese. Omit mint leaves and chives in dressing.

Roasted Cauliflower

A tasty way to cook cauliflower. Roasting brings out a wonderful earthy flavour.

Cauliflower florets	**6 cups**	**1.5 L**
Canola oil	**1 1/2 tbsp.**	**25 mL**
Ground nutmeg	**1/2 tsp.**	**2 mL**
Garlic powder	**1/4 tsp.**	**1 mL**
Pepper	**1/4 tsp.**	**1 mL**

Toss all 5 ingredients in large bowl. Spread on greased baking sheet. Bake in 375°F (190ºC) oven for about 30 minutes until cauliflower is tender-crisp. Makes 4 cups (1 L).

NUTRITION INFORMATION 1 cup (250 mL): 87 Calories; 5.6 g Total Fat (3.1 g Mono, 1.7 g Poly, 0.5 g Sat); 0 mg Cholesterol; 8 g Carbohydrate; 3 g Fibre; 3 g Protein; 48 mg Sodium

CHOICES 1/2 Fruit & Vegetable; 1/2 Protein; 1 Fat & Oil

Pictured on page 125.

Potato And Fennel Bake

Fennel and potatoes baked with fresh dill and Parmesan cheese. A unique and elegant way to serve potatoes with the Sunday roast.

Large potatoes, peeled and cut crosswise into 1/4 inch (6 mm) thick slices	**3**	**3**
Large fennel bulb (white part only), trimmed and thinly sliced	**1**	**1**
Chopped fresh dill (or 1 1/4 tsp., 6 mL, dill weed)	**1 1/2 tbsp.**	**25 mL**
Low-sodium prepared chicken broth	**1/2 cup**	**125 mL**
Milk	**1/2 cup**	**125 mL**
Finely grated fresh Parmesan cheese	**3 tbsp.**	**50 mL**
Chopped fresh dill (or 1 1/4 tsp., 6 mL, dill weed)	**1 1/2 tbsp.**	**25 mL**
Pepper	**1/2 tsp.**	**2 mL**

Arrange 1/2 of potato in lightly greased shallow 3 quart (3 L) casserole. Lay 1/2 of fennel over potato.

Sprinkle with first amount of dill. Layer with remaining potatoes and fennel.

(continued on next page)

Combine broth and milk in 1 cup (250 mL) liquid measure. Pour over potato mixture.

Sprinkle with Parmesan cheese, second amount of dill and pepper. Cover. Bake in 350°F (175°C) oven for 30 minutes. Remove cover. Bake, uncovered, for about 30 minutes until potato is tender and top is browned. Serves 8.

NUTRITION INFORMATION 1 serving: 68 Calories; 1 g Total Fat (0.3 g Mono, 0.1 g Poly, 0.6 g Sat); 3 mg Cholesterol; 12 g Carbohydrate; 2 g Fibre; 3 g Protein; 111 mg Sodium

CHOICES 1/2 Starch; 1/2 Milk

Mashed Sweet Potatoes

This smooth, creamy purée has flecks of green parsley.

Canola oil	**2 tsp.**	**10 mL**
Thinly sliced onion	**1 cup**	**250 mL**
Chopped sweet potatoes	**4 cups**	**1 L**
Water		
Salt	**1/4 tsp.**	**1 mL**
Low-fat plain yogurt	**2 – 3 tbsp.**	**30 – 50 mL**
Chopped fresh parsley (or 3/4 – 1 1/2 tsp., 4 – 7 mL, flakes)	**1 – 2 tbsp.**	**15 – 30 mL**

Heat canola oil in medium frying pan on medium. Add onion. Cook for about 15 minutes, stirring often, until onion is softened.

Cook sweet potatoes in water and salt in medium saucepan on medium-high for about 15 minutes until tender. Drain well. Return to saucepan. Mash until no lumps remain.

Add yogurt, parsley and onion mixture. Stir well. Makes 2 1/2 cups (625 mL).

NUTRITION INFORMATION 1/2 cup (125 mL): 151 Calories; 2.3 g Total Fat (1.1 g Mono, 0.7 g Poly, 0.2 g Sat); 0 mg Cholesterol; 31 g Carbohydrate; 4 g Fibre; 3 g Protein; 21 mg Sodium

CHOICES 1 1/2 Starch; 1/2 Fruit & Vegetable; 1/2 Fat & Oil

Maple Butternut Squash

A comforting, colourful side dish that is a great accompaniment to stew or even warm in a fresh green salad. Peppery and vibrant, with a hint of rosemary.

Cubed butternut squash	**5 cups**	**1.25 L**
Canola oil	**2 tsp.**	**10 mL**
Garlic cloves, bruised (see Note)	**2**	**2**
Sprigs of fresh rosemary	**2**	**2**
Salt	**1/4 tsp.**	**1 mL**
Pepper	**1/4 tsp.**	**1 mL**
Maple (or maple-flavoured) syrup	**1 tbsp.**	**15 mL**

Put first 6 ingredients into large bowl. Toss until evenly coated. Transfer to greased baking sheet. Bake, uncovered, in 400°F (205°C) oven for about 40 minutes, stirring once, until starting to brown on edges. Discard rosemary sprigs.

Drizzle with maple syrup. Toss. Bake for about 10 minutes until glazed and golden. Makes 2 cups (500 mL).

NUTRITION INFORMATION 1/2 cup (125 mL): 119 Calories; 2.5 g Total Fat (1.4 g Mono, 0.8 g Poly, 0.2 g Sat); 0 mg Cholesterol; 26 g Carbohydrate; 3 g Fibre; 2 g Protein; 156 mg Sodium

CHOICES 1 1/2 Starch; 1/2 Fat & Oil

Pictured on page 125.

Note: To bruise garlic cloves, hit cloves with a mallet or the flat side of a wide knife to "bruise" or crack them open slightly.

Kid-Friendly Idea

Omit garlic cloves and rosemary.

Zucchini Pepper Combo

Tender-crisp, perfectly cooked vegetables. All the "juices" form a tasty sauce. Simplicity in seasoning and cooking brings out the best flavour of these vegetables.

Medium zucchini (with peel), quartered lengthwise and seeded	2	2
Olive (or canola) oil	2 tsp.	10 mL
Red medium pepper, diced	1	1
Yellow or orange medium pepper, diced	1	1
Lemon pepper	1/2 tsp.	2 mL
Balsamic vinegar	2 tsp.	10 mL
Pepper, sprinkle		

Cut quartered zucchini crosswise into 1/2 inch (12 mm) pieces.

Heat olive oil in large non-stick frying pan or wok on medium-high. Add zucchini, red and yellow peppers and lemon pepper. Stir-fry for 5 to 7 minutes until tender-crisp and starting to turn golden.

Sprinkle with balsamic vinegar and pepper. Stir. Serve immediately. Makes 3 cups (750 mL).

NUTRITION INFORMATION 1/2 cup (125 mL): 36 Calories; 1.7 g Total Fat (1.1 g Mono, 0.2 g Poly, 0.2 g Sat); 0 mg Cholesterol; 5 g Carbohydrate; 2 g Fibre; 1 g Protein; 3 mg Sodium

CHOICES 1/2 Fruit & Vegetable; 1/2 Fat & Oil

Pictured on page 18.

Kid-Friendly Idea

Omit the balsamic vinegar and sprinkle of pepper. Substitute with 2 tsp. (10 mL) low-fat Italian dressing.

NUTRITION INFORMATION 1 serving: 37 Calories; 1.8 g Total Fat (1.2 g Mono, 0.2 g Poly, 0.2 g Sat); 0 mg Cholesterol; 5 g Carbohydrate; 2 g Fibre; 1 g Protein; 27 mg Sodium

CHOICES 1/2 Fruit & Vegetable; 1/2 Fat & Oi

Creamy Spinach

Fast and easy with lots of flavour. Goes well with grilled chicken or beef.

Hard margarine (or butter)	**2 tsp.**	**10 mL**
Finely chopped onion	**1 cup**	**250 mL**
Garlic clove, minced (or 1/4 tsp., 1 mL, powder)	**1**	**1**
Fresh spinach, stems removed, lightly packed	**6 cups**	**1.5 L**
Ground nutmeg	**1/4 tsp.**	**1 mL**
Lemon pepper	**1/4 tsp.**	**1 mL**
Light sour cream	**2 tbsp.**	**30 mL**

Melt margarine in large frying pan on medium. Add onion and garlic. Cook for 5 to 10 minutes, stirring often, until onion is softened.

Add spinach. Heat and stir for about 3 minutes until spinach is almost wilted.

Add nutmeg, lemon pepper and sour cream. Heat and stir until sour cream is combined. Makes about 1 1/2 cups (375 mL).

NUTRITION INFORMATION 1/2 cup (125 mL): 82 Calories; 3.8 g Total Fat (2.1 g Mono, 0.5 g Poly, 1.5 g Sat); 2 mg Cholesterol; 10 g Carbohydrate; 4 g Fibre; 4 g Protein; 130 mg Sodium

CHOICES 1/2 Fruit & Vegetable; 1/2 Protein; 1/2 Fat & Oil

1. Spinach And Pork Salad, page 79
2. Grilled Pork Sandwich, page 78

Asparagus And Mushrooms

Tender-crisp, green asparagus is tasty with a fresh lemon flavour and honey sweetness. An elegant presentation.

Hard margarine (or butter)	2 tsp.	10 mL
Sliced fresh white mushrooms	2 cups	500 mL
Fresh asparagus, trimmed of tough ends	1 lb.	454 g
Chopped fresh parsley (or 2 1/4 tsp., 11 mL, flakes)	3 tbsp.	50 mL
Liquid honey	2 tsp.	10 mL
Finely grated lemon zest	1/4 tsp.	1 mL
Salt	1/4 tsp.	1 mL

Melt margarine in large frying pan on medium-high. Add mushrooms and asparagus. Heat for about 5 minutes, stirring occasionally, until asparagus is tender-crisp.

Add remaining 4 ingredients. Heat and stir for about 30 seconds until well combined. Serves 4 to 6.

NUTRITION INFORMATION 1 serving: 63 Calories; 2.3 g Total Fat (1.3 g Mono, 0.4 g Poly, 0.5 g Sat); 0 mg Cholesterol; 10 g Carbohydrate; 2 g Fibre; 3 g Protein; 176 mg Sodium

CHOICES 1 Fruit & Vegetable; 1/2 Fat & Oil

Pictured on page 36.

1. Crunchy Rice Salad, page 96
2. Potato Salad, page 101
3. Creamed Veggie Spaghetti, page 94

Pea Medley

Sweet, tender-crisp peas glazed with butter and fresh mint. Delightful mint flavour goes so well with peas.

Low-sodium prepared chicken broth (or water)	**2 tbsp.**	**30 mL**
Green onions, cut into 1 inch (2.5 cm) pieces	**8**	**8**
Garlic clove, minced (or 1/4 tsp., 1 mL, powder)	**1**	**1**
Package of sugar snap peas (about 2 cups, 500 mL)	**8 oz.**	**227 g**
Fresh snow peas	**2 cups**	**500 mL**
Frozen peas	**1 cup**	**250 mL**
Salt, sprinkle		
Pepper, sprinkle		
Chopped fresh mint (not dried)	**2 tbsp.**	**30 mL**
Hard margarine (or butter)	**2 tsp.**	**10 mL**

Heat broth in wok or large frying pan on medium-high. Add green onion and garlic. Stir-fry for about 1 minute until fragrant.

Add next 5 ingredients. Cook, uncovered, for 2 to 3 minutes, stirring often, until peas are tender-crisp. Do not overcook.

Add mint and margarine. Stir-fry for about 30 seconds until margarine is melted and peas are coated. Serve immediately. Makes 4 cups (1 L).

NUTRITION INFORMATION 2/3 cup (150 mL): 62 Calories; 1.5 g Total Fat (0.9 g Mono, 0.2 g Poly, 0.3 g Sat); 0 mg Cholesterol; 9 g Carbohydrate; 3 g Fibre; 3 g Protein; 60 mg Sodium

CHOICES 1/2 Starch; 1/2 Protein

Pictured on page 125.

Kid-Friendly Idea

Omit garlic and mint.

Spaghetti Squash Casserole

Thick, creamy and cheesy! A good accompaniment to roast beef, pork or chicken.

Medium spaghetti squash (about 3 – 3 1/2 lbs., 1.4 – 1.6 kg), halved lengthwise and seeds removed	1	1
Boiling water		
Olive (or canola) oil	2 tsp.	10 mL
Large sweet onion (such as Vidalia), thinly sliced	1	1
Low-sodium prepared chicken broth	1/2 cup	125 mL
Light sour cream	1/2 cup	125 mL
Grated light Monterey Jack cheese	3/4 cup	175 mL
Pepper, sprinkle		
Grated light Monterey Jack cheese	3/4 cup	175 mL
Low-fat herb-flavoured croutons, coarsely crushed	1/2 cup	125 mL
Chopped fresh parsley (or 3/4 tsp., 4 mL, flakes)	1 tbsp.	15 mL

Place squash, cut sides down, in ungreased 3 quart (3 L) casserole or medium roaster. Add about 2 inches (5 cm) boiling water. Cover. Bake in 375°F (190°C) oven for about 30 minutes until tender. Drain. Place, cut sides up, on wire rack until cool enough to handle. Scrape squash with fork to remove strands into greased 2 quart (2 L) casserole. Makes about 5 cups (1.25 L) squash.

Heat olive oil in large non-stick frying pan or wok on medium-high. Add onion. Cook for about 10 minutes, stirring often, adding chicken broth in small amounts, until onion is softened and golden brown. Add to squash. Toss.

Add sour cream, first amount of cheese and pepper. Mix well. Pat down gently and evenly.

Toss second amount of cheese, croutons and parsley in small bowl.

Sprinkle over casserole. Bake, uncovered, in 350°F (175°C) oven for about 45 minutes until bubbling around edges and browned. A knife inserted into centre for 30 seconds should come out hot to touch. Makes about 6 cups (1.5 L).

NUTRITION INFORMATION 1/2 cup (125 mL): 91 Calories; 4.6 g Total Fat (1.9 g Mono, 0.3 g Poly, 2.7 g Sat); 10 mg Cholesterol; 8 g Carbohydrate; 1 g Fibre; 5 g Protein; 144 mg Sodium

CHOICES 1/2 Fruit & Vegetable; 1/2 Protein; 1/2 Fat & Oil

To Make Ahead: Prepare to final baking stage. Cover. Chill until ready to use. Bake in 350°F (175°C) oven for about 1 hour.

Oven-Fried Vegetables

Enjoy these for the taste of deep-fried vegetables without the fat. These crisp mixed vegetables are lightly breaded and baked. Serve with Spicy Roasted Pepper Sauce, page 113, as a dip. Use a variety of your favourite vegetables.

Frozen egg product, thawed (see Egg Note, below)	1/2 cup	125 mL
Blanched or partially cooked mixed vegetable pieces (see Blanched Note, below)	2 lbs.	900 g
Fine cornflake crumbs	1 cup	250 mL
Garlic and herb no-salt seasoning (such as Mrs. Dash)	1 1/2 tsp.	7 mL

Put egg product into large bowl. Add vegetables. Stir until coated.

Combine crumbs and seasoning in large resealable freezer bag. Add vegetables, in small batches. Shake until coated. Arrange in single layer on greased baking sheet. Spray vegetables with cooking spray until well coated. Bake in 400°F (205°C) oven for about 20 minutes until browned. Makes about 6 cups (1.5 L). Serves 6 to 8.

NUTRITION INFORMATION 1 serving: 137 Calories; 2.1 g Total Fat (0.4 g Mono, 1.1 g Poly, 0.4 g Sat); trace Cholesterol; 25 g Carbohydrate; 3 g Fibre; 5 g Protein; 224 mg Sodium

CHOICES 2 1/2 Fruit & Vegetable; 1/2 Protein

Pictured on page 125.

Egg Note: 1/4 cup (60 mL) frozen egg product is equivalent to 1 large egg. Recipe needs 1/2 cup (125 mL) egg product to coat vegetables, however, about 2 tbsp. (30 mL) will be discarded from bottom of bowl after coating.

Blanched Note: Blanch broccoli and cauliflower florets, bell pepper pieces and zucchini spears in boiling water for 1 minute and then plunge into ice water. Partially cook hard vegetables (such as halved baby potatoes, peeled winter squash and turnip chunks, and carrot and parsnip pieces) by boiling or steaming for 3 to 5 minutes until just barely tender, and then plunging into ice water.

Spicy Roasted Pepper Sauce

A thick sauce with a hint of jalapeño. Serve with chicken, beef or lamb, or toss through pasta. Can also be used as a pizza sauce or dip. If you prefer a hotter sauce, leave the seeds in the jalapeño pepper.

Red medium peppers, quartered, seeds and ribs removed	6	6
Medium onions, cut lengthwise into wedges	2	2
Garlic cloves	2	2
Medium jalapeño pepper, seeds and ribs removed (see Tip, below)	1	1
Olive (or canola) oil	1 tbsp.	15 mL
Brown sugar, packed	1 tsp.	5 mL
Salt, sprinkle		
Pepper, sprinkle		

Combine all 8 ingredients on large greased baking sheet. Bake in 375ºF (190ºC) oven for about 1 hour, stirring occasionally, until pepper and onion are soft and browned. Cool. Process in blender or food processor until smooth. Makes about 3 cups (750 mL).

NUTRITION INFORMATION 1/4 cup (60 mL): 43 Calories; 1.3 g Total Fat (0.9 g Mono, 0.2 g Poly, 0.2 g Sat); 0 mg Cholesterol; 8 g Carbohydrate; 2 g Fibre; 1 g Protein; 3 mg Sodium

CHOICES 1/2 Fruit & Vegetable

Pictured on page 36.

Kid-Friendly Idea

Omit the jalapeño pepper.

Wear rubber gloves when cutting jalapeño peppers and avoid touching your eyes.

Roasted Tomato Sauce

This sweet tomato, basil and garlic sauce has a wonderfully thick consistency. Good served with barbecued meat or tossed through pasta. Leftover sauce can for be frozen for later use.

Roma (plum) tomatoes (about 2 1/4 lbs., 1 kg), halved	15	15
Sweet (or regular) chili sauce	2 tbsp.	30 mL
Chopped fresh basil (or 1 1/2 tsp., 7 mL, dried)	2 tbsp.	30 mL
Tomato paste (see Tip, page 43)	1 tbsp.	15 mL
White wine vinegar	1 tbsp.	15 mL
Olive (or canola) oil	2 tsp.	10 mL
Garlic clove, minced (or 1/4 tsp., 1 mL, powder)	1	1
Salt	1/4 tsp.	1 mL

Place tomatoes, cut side up, on greased baking sheet. Brush with chili sauce. Bake in 375ºF (190ºC) oven for about 45 minutes until tomatoes are soft and lightly browned on edges. Let stand on baking sheet for 10 minutes to cool.

Process tomatoes and remaining 6 ingredients in blender or food processor until smooth. Makes about 3 cups (750 mL).

NUTRITION INFORMATION 1/4 cup (60 mL): 44 Calories; 1.3 g Total Fat (0.5 g Mono, 0.4 g Poly, 0.1 g Sat); 0 mg Cholesterol; 8 g Carbohydrate; 2 g Fibre; 1 g Protein; 103 mg Sodium

CHOICES 1/2 Fruit & Vegetable

Lightened-Up Cheese Sauce

This creamy cheese sauce has a sharp cheese flavour. Great on steamed vegetables, potatoes or an egg white omelet.

Skim milk	1 1/4 cups	300 mL
All-purpose flour	3 tbsp.	50 mL
Grated light sharp Cheddar cheese	1 1/2 cups	375 mL
Non-fat spreadable garlic-herb cream cheese	1/4 cup	60 mL
Seasoned salt	1/2 tsp.	2 mL
Dry mustard	1/4 tsp.	1 mL
Paprika	1/4 tsp.	1 mL

(continued on next page)

Stir milk into flour in medium saucepan until smooth. Heat and stir on medium until boiling and thickened. Reduce heat to low.

Add remaining 5 ingredients. Heat and stir until both cheeses are melted. Makes 2 cups (500 mL).

NUTRITION INFORMATION 1/4 cup (60 mL): 101 Calories; 4.6 g Total Fat (1.4 g Mono, 0.1 g Poly, 2.9 g Sat); 14 mg Cholesterol; 6 g Carbohydrate; trace Fibre; 8 g Protein; 239 mg Sodium

CHOICES 1 Milk; 1/2 Protein

Onion And Garlic Dipping Sauce

The perfect sauce for dipping vegetables. Makes a great topping for a baked potato as well. Excellent with Spice Blackened Snapper, page 27.

Light sour cream	**2/3 cup**	**150 mL**
Ultra low-fat mayonnaise	**1/3 cup**	**75 mL**
Garlic cloves	**3**	**3**
Lemon juice	**2 tbsp.**	**30 mL**
Olive oil	**1 tbsp.**	**15 mL**
Finely grated lemon zest	**1/4 tsp.**	**1 mL**
Green onions, finely chopped	**2**	**2**

Process first 6 ingredients in blender or food processor, scraping down sides as necessary, until smooth. Pour into small bowl.

Stir in green onion. Cover. Chill for 30 minutes to blend flavours. Makes 1 cup (250 mL).

NUTRITION INFORMATION 2 tbsp. (30 mL): 36 Calories; 3 g Total Fat (2 g Mono, 0.2 g Poly, 1.9 g Sat); 4 mg Cholesterol; 2 g Carbohydrate; trace Fibre; 1 g Protein; 70 mg Sodium

CHOICES 1/2 Fat & Oil

Creamy Mushroom Sauce

A creamy, golden-brown sauce that mushroom lovers will adore! Perfect over steak or chicken.

Canola oil	**1 tbsp.**	**15 mL**
Sliced fresh brown (or white) mushrooms	**2 cups**	**500 mL**
Hard margarine (or butter)	**1 tbsp.**	**15 mL**
Garlic clove, minced (or 1/4 tsp., 1 mL, powder)	**1**	**1**
All-purpose flour	**1 tbsp.**	**15 mL**
Low-sodium prepared chicken (or vegetable) broth	**1 cup**	**250 mL**
Dry white (or alcohol-free) wine	**1/2 cup**	**125 mL**
Light sour cream	**2 tbsp.**	**30 mL**
Chopped fresh chives (or 1 1/2 tsp., 7 mL, dried)	**2 tbsp.**	**30 mL**
Salt, sprinkle		
Pepper, sprinkle		

Heat canola oil in large frying pan on medium. Add mushrooms. Cook for about 5 minutes, stirring occasionally, until lightly browned. Remove to small bowl.

Add margarine and garlic to same frying pan. Heat and stir on medium for about 1 minute until garlic is fragrant. Add flour. Heat and stir for 1 minute.

Add mushrooms, broth and wine. Cook and stir for about 5 minutes until boiling and thickened.

Add remaining 4 ingredients. Heat and stir for about 2 minutes until well combined. Makes about 1 1/4 cups (300 mL).

NUTRITION INFORMATION 2 tbsp. (30 mL): 41 Calories; 2.7 g Total Fat (1.6 g Mono, 0.6 g Poly, 0.6 g Sat); 1 mg Cholesterol; 2 g Carbohydrate; trace Fibre; 1 g Protein; 77 mg Sodium

CHOICES 1/2 Fat & Oil

Tropical Yogurt Topping

This creamy topping has a wonderful banana flavour. Delicious on burgers or sandwiches.

Plain yogurt, drained (see Note)	**3/4 cup**	**175 mL**
Brown sugar, packed	**1 tbsp.**	**15 mL**
Dark rum (or 1/2 tsp., 2 mL, rum flavouring)	**1 tbsp.**	**15 mL**
Lemon juice	**2 tsp.**	**10 mL**
Salt	**1/4 tsp.**	**1 mL**

(continued on next page)

Can of pineapple slices, drained and diced	**14 oz.**	**398 mL**
Chopped fresh parsley (or 2 1/4 tsp., 11 mL, flakes)	**3 tbsp.**	**50 mL**
Medium bananas, diced	**2**	**2**

Combine first 5 ingredients in medium bowl. Stir until sugar is dissolved.

Add pineapple and parsley. Stir.

Fold in banana gently until coated. Makes 2 1/4 cups (550 mL).

NUTRITION INFORMATION 1/4 cup (60 mL): 58 Calories; 0.5 g Total Fat (0.1 g Mono, 0 g Poly, 0.3 g Sat); 1 mg Cholesterol; 12 g Carbohydrate; 1 g Fibre; 2 g Protein; 83 mg Sodium

CHOICES 1 Fruit & Vegetable

Variation: Omit chopped fresh parsley. Use same amount of finely chopped fresh mint.

Apple Cranberry Chutney

This chutney is great with pork or roasted turkey. Make ahead of time and freeze in an airtight container.

Chopped, peeled tart cooking apples (such as Granny Smith), about 1 1/2 lbs. (680 g)	**5 cups**	**1.25 L**
Dried cranberries	**1 cup**	**250 mL**
White wine vinegar	**1/2 cup**	**125 mL**
Apple juice	**1/2 cup**	**125 mL**
Brown sugar, packed	**1/4 cup**	**60 mL**
Cinnamon stick (4 inch, 10 cm, length)	**1**	**1**
Ground ginger	**1/2 tsp.**	**2 mL**
Ground cloves	**1/16 tsp.**	**0.5 mL**
Salt	**1/4 tsp.**	**1 mL**

Combine all 9 ingredients in large uncovered pot or Dutch oven. Heat and stir on medium until sugar is dissolved. Bring to a boil. Reduce heat to medium-low. Simmer, uncovered, for about 40 minutes, stirring occasionally, until thickened and most liquid is evaporated. Remove and discard cinnamon stick. Makes about 3 1/4 cups (800 mL).

NUTRITION INFORMATION 2 tbsp. (30 mL): 24 Calories; trace Total Fat (0 g Mono, 0 g Poly, 0 g Sat); 0 mg Cholesterol; 6 g Carbohydrate; trace Fibre; trace Protein; 23 mg Sodium

CHOICES 1/2 Fruit & Vegetable

Pictured on page 53.

Apricot Clafouti

Pronounced kla-FOO-tee. A cobbler-like dessert that is equally as good with cherries, plums or peaches in place of apricots. Sprinkle top with sliced almonds for a subtle nutty flavour and texture.

All-purpose flour	1/2 cup	125 mL
Whole wheat flour	2 tbsp.	30 mL
Granulated sugar	1/3 cup	75 mL
Buttermilk (or reconstituted from powder)	1 3/4 cups	425 mL
Frozen egg product, thawed (see Note)	1 cup	250 mL
Ground nutmeg	1/2 tsp.	2 mL
Can of apricot halves, drained	14 oz.	398 mL

Combine both flours and sugar in large bowl.

Combine buttermilk, egg product and nutmeg in medium bowl. Pour over flour mixture. Whisk until smooth.

Cut each apricot piece in half. Arrange apricots in bottom of greased 9 inch (22 cm) pie plate. Carefully pour batter over apricots. Bake in 350°F (175°C) oven for 40 to 45 minutes until set. Serve warm or at room temperature. Serves 6 to 8.

NUTRITION INFORMATION 1 serving: 211 Calories; 5.7 g Total Fat (1.3 g Mono, 2.8 g Poly, 1.3 g Sat); 3 mg Cholesterol; 31 g Carbohydrate; 2 g Fibre; 9 g Protein; 166 mg Sodium

CHOICES 1/2 Starch; 1/2 Fruit & Vegetable; 1 Milk; 1/2 Protein; 1/2 Fat & Oil; 1 Sugar

Note: 3 tbsp. (50 mL) frozen egg product, thawed, is equivalent to 1 large egg.

Blueberry Cobbler

A warm, comforting, old-fashioned dessert. Serve with low-fat ice cream, frozen yogurt or low-fat custard for a special treat.

Hard margarine (or butter), melted	**1/4 cup**	**60 mL**
All-purpose flour	**1 cup**	**250 mL**
Milk	**3/4 cup**	**175 mL**
Granulated sugar	**2 tbsp.**	**30 mL**
Baking powder	**2 tsp.**	**10 mL**
Vanilla	**1 tsp.**	**5 mL**
Ground cinnamon	**1/2 tsp.**	**2 mL**
Ground nutmeg	**1/4 tsp.**	**1 mL**
Fresh (or frozen, thawed) blueberries	**2 cups**	**500 mL**
Granulated sugar	**2 tbsp.**	**30 mL**
Finely grated lemon zest	**1 tsp.**	**5 mL**
Water	**1/2 cup**	**125 mL**

Pour margarine into bottom of lightly greased 1 1/2 quart (1.5 L) casserole.

Combine next 7 ingredients in medium bowl. Dollop evenly over margarine.

Combine blueberries, second amount of sugar and zest in medium bowl. Sprinkle over flour mixture.

Drizzle with water. Do not stir. Bake, uncovered, in 350°F (175ºC) oven for 40 to 45 minutes until bubbling and lightly browned. Serves 6.

NUTRITION INFORMATION 1 serving: 232 Calories; 8.9 g Total Fat (5.4 g Mono, 0.9 g Poly, 1.9 g Sat); 1 mg Cholesterol; 35 g Carbohydrate; 2 g Fibre; 4 g Protein; 238 mg Sodium

CHOICES 1 Starch; 1 Fruit & Vegetable; 2 Fat & Oil; 2 Sugar

FRUIT COBBLER: Substitute the same amount of your favourite fresh (or frozen, thawed and drained) fruit for the blueberries.

Strawberry Shortcakes

Deliciously light and airy tea biscuits topped with your favourite jam.

BUTTERMILK TEA BISCUITS

All-purpose flour	**1 1/2 cups**	**375 mL**
Baking powder	**2 tsp.**	**10 mL**
Salt, just a pinch		
Hard margarine (or butter)	**2 tbsp.**	**30 mL**
Buttermilk (or reconstituted from powder)	**3/4 cup**	**175 mL**
Salt, just a pinch		
Sugar-free strawberry jam	**1/3 cup**	**75 mL**
Low-fat plain yogurt	**1/3 cup**	**75 mL**
Fresh strawberries, quartered (optional)	**2**	**2**

Buttermilk Tea Biscuits: Combine flour, baking powder and first amount of salt in medium bowl. Cut in margarine until mixture resembles coarse crumbs.

Add buttermilk and second amount of salt. Stir until just moistened. Do not overmix. Let stand for 10 minutes. Lightly press out dough on lightly floured surface to 1 inch (2.5 cm) thickness. Cut out circles from dough using lightly floured 2 inch (5 cm) cookie cutter. Arrange circles in single layer, almost touching, in lightly greased 9 x 9 inch (22 x 22 cm) pan. Bake in 450°F (230°C) oven for 10 to 12 minutes until well risen and lightly browned on top and bottom. Let stand in pan for 5 minutes before removing to wire rack to cool. Makes 8 biscuits.

Carefully split each biscuit in half. Place 2 halves, cut side up, on each of 8 dessert plates. Spread each side with jam. Top with small dollop of yogurt and strawberry quarter. Makes 16 biscuit halves. Serves 8.

NUTRITION INFORMATION 1 serving: 143 Calories; 3.5 g Total Fat (2 g Mono, 0.4 g Poly, 0.9 g Sat); 2 mg Cholesterol; 23 g Carbohydrate; trace Fibre; 4 g Protein; 160 mg Sodium

CHOICES 1 Starch; 1 Fruit & Vegetable; 1/2 Fat & Oil

Pictured on page 126.

Tropical Trifles

Kids and adults alike will love these attractive individual desserts. A wonderful combination of colours, flavours and textures.

Package of sugar-free lime-flavoured jelly powder (4 serving size)	**1/3 oz.**	**10 g**
Vanilla wafers, coarsely crushed	**12**	**12**
Can of pineapple tidbits, drained	**14 oz.**	**398 mL**
Low-fat tropical fruit yogurt	**1 cup**	**250 mL**
Toasted sliced almonds (see Tip, page 63), optional	**2 tbsp.**	**30 mL**

Prepare jelly powder according to package directions. Transfer to 9 x 9 inch (22 x 22 cm) pan. Spread in even layer. Chill until set. Cut into cubes.

Divide and spoon crushed wafers into bottom of 6 individual 9 oz. (255 mL) serving glasses. Top with pineapple, jelly and yogurt.

Sprinkle tops with almonds. Serves 6.

NUTRITION INFORMATION 1 serving: 121 Calories; 2.4 g Total Fat (0.9 g Mono, 0.5 g Poly, 0.8 g Sat); 9 mg Cholesterol; 22 g Carbohydrate; trace Fibre; 4 g Protein; 94 mg Sodium

CHOICES 1 Starch; 1/2 Fruit & Vegetable; 1/2 Fat & Oil

Pictured on front cover.

Buttermilk Pancakes And Apples

Tender, sweet apple pieces in a warm maple syrup sauce. Delicious, but serve as an occasional treat.

APPLE TOPPING

Tart medium apples (such as Granny Smith), peeled, cored and quartered	4	4
Apple juice	1 cup	250 mL
Maple (or maple-flavoured) syrup	2 tbsp.	30 mL
Ground cinnamon	1/4 tsp.	1 mL

PANCAKES

All-purpose (or whole wheat) flour	1 1/2 cups	375 mL
Baking powder	1 tbsp.	15 mL
Large eggs	2	2
Buttermilk (or reconstituted from powder)	1 1/4 cups	300 mL
Vanilla	1 tsp.	5 mL

Apple Topping: Slice apple quarters in half lengthwise. Combine apple, apple juice, maple syrup and cinnamon in large frying pan. Heat on medium for about 15 minutes, stirring occasionally, until apples are softened but not broken down, and sauce is slightly thickened. Keep warm. Makes 2 cups (500 mL) topping.

Pancakes: Combine flour and baking powder in large bowl. Make a well in centre.

Beat eggs, buttermilk and vanilla in small bowl. Add to well. Stir until just moistened. Heat large non-stick frying pan on medium. Spray lightly with cooking spray. Pour 1/3 cup (75 mL) batter into pan for each pancake. Cook for about 1 minute until bubbles appear on top and edges are dry. Flip. Cook for 1 to 2 minutes until golden. Makes 8 pancakes. Serve topping over pancakes. Serves 4.

NUTRITION INFORMATION 1 serving: 386 Calories; 4.2 g Total Fat (1.2 g Mono, 0.7 g Poly, 1.4 g Sat); 111 mg Cholesterol; 77 g Carbohydrate; 4 g Fibre; 11 g Protein; 398 mg Sodium

CHOICES 2 1/2 Starch; 3 Fruit & Vegetable; 1/2 Milk; 1/2 Fat & Oil

Pictured on page 126.

Pear And Yogurt Freeze

A pretty, pale pink "ice" with a hint of pear. Dress up by serving in glass bowls and garnishing with a sprig of mint.

Envelope of unflavoured gelatin	1/4 oz.	7 g
Cans of pear halves (14 oz., 398 mL, each), drained and juice reserved	2	2
Non-fat berry yogurt (your choice)	1 1/2 cups	375 mL

Sprinkle gelatin over 1/2 cup (125 mL) reserved pear juice in small saucepan. Let stand for 1 minute. Heat and stir on medium until gelatin is dissolved. Add remaining reserved pear juice. Stir.

Process gelatin mixture, pears and yogurt in blender or food processor until smooth. Pour into ungreased 9 x 13 inch (22 x 33 cm) pan. Freeze, uncovered, for 2 hours. Scrape into large bowl. Beat on high until smooth and slushy. Pour into 1 1/2 quart (1.5 L) airtight container. Freeze until firm. Let stand at room temperature for about 15 minutes before serving. Makes 5 cups (1.25 L).

NUTRITION INFORMATION 1/2 cup (125 mL): 68 Calories; 0.1 g Total Fat (0 g Mono, 0 g Poly, 0.1 g Sat); 1 mg Cholesterol; 15 g Carbohydrate; 2 g Fibre; 3 g Protein; 32 mg Sodium

CHOICES 1 Fruit & Vegetable; 1/2 Milk

Pictured on page 126.

Peanut Butter Banana Shake

A delicious, creamy shake—perfect for a breakfast on the run or a quick snack.

Fat-free sour cream	2/3 cup	150 mL
Medium bananas, sliced	2	2
Light smooth peanut butter	2 tbsp.	30 mL
Ice cubes	3	3

Process sour cream, banana and peanut butter in blender until smooth.

With motor running, add ice cubes through hole in lid. Process until thick and smooth. Makes 2 cups (500 mL).

NUTRITION INFORMATION 1 cup (250 mL): 291 Calories; 7 Total Fat (2.9 g Mono, 2.3 g Poly, 1.4 g Sat); 0 mg Cholesterol; 49 g Carbohydrate; 3 g Fibre; 4 g Protein; 88 mg Sodium

CHOICES 1 Starch; 3 Fruit & Vegetable; 1 1/2 Fat & Oil

Piñana Milk Smoothie

A smooth, creamy beverage with a refreshing tropical flavour. Great for a quick breakfast or a healthy snack.

Frozen banana, sliced	1	1
Pineapple juice	1 cup	250 mL
Milk	1 cup	250 mL
Vanilla	1/2 tsp.	2 mL

Process all 4 ingredients in blender or food processor until smooth. Serve over ice cubes in tall glasses. Makes 2 1/2 cups (625 mL).

NUTRITION INFORMATION 3/4 cup (175 mL): 111 Calories; 1.1 g Total Fat (0.3 g Mono, 0.1 g Poly, 0.6 g Sat); 3 mg Cholesterol; 23 g Carbohydrate; 1 g Fibre; 3 g Protein; 40 mg Sodium

CHOICES 2 Fruit & Vegetable; 1/2 Milk

Pictured on page 144.

HAWAIIAN SMOOTHIE: Omit vanilla. Add 1 tsp. (5 mL) coconut extract.

1. Roasted Cauliflower, page 102
2. Pea Medley, page 110
3. Maple Butternut Squash, page 104
4. Oven-Fried Vegetables, page 112

Strawberry Orange Smoothie

A creamy drink with refreshing strawberry and orange flavours. A great mid-morning or mid-afternoon pick-me-up.

Milk	**1 cup**	**250 mL**
Frozen vanilla yogurt	**1/2 cup**	**125 mL**
Frozen concentrated orange juice	**1/4 cup**	**60 mL**
Large fresh strawberries	**8**	**8**

Process all 4 ingredients in blender or food processor for about 30 seconds until smooth. Makes 3 cups (750 mL).

NUTRITION INFORMATION 3/4 cup (175 mL): 100 Calories; 1.5 g Total Fat (0.4 g Mono, 0.1 g Poly, 0.8 g Sat); 4 mg Cholesterol; 18 g Carbohydrate; 1 g Fibre; 4 g Protein; 52 mg Sodium

CHOICES 1 Fruit & Vegetable; 1 Milk

Pictured on page 144.

Variation: Use frozen strawberries instead of fresh. With blender motor running, drop frozen strawberries, 1 at a time, through hole in lid until mixture is thick and smooth.

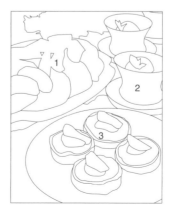

1. Buttermilk Pancakes And Apples, page 122
2. Pear And Yogurt Freeze, page 123
3. Strawberry Shortcakes, page 120

Corn Muffin Surprise

A ribbon of strawberry jam runs through these tasty muffins.

Yellow cornmeal	**1 cup**	**250 mL**
Buttermilk (or reconstituted from powder)	**1 cup**	**250 mL**
Whole wheat flour	**1/2 cup**	**125 mL**
All-purpose flour	**1/2 cup**	**125 mL**
Brown sugar, packed	**2 tbsp.**	**30 mL**
Baking powder	**1 tbsp.**	**15 mL**
Salt	**1/4 tsp.**	**1 mL**
Large egg	**1**	**1**
Canola oil	**2 tbsp.**	**30 mL**
Unsweetened strawberry jam (or fruit spread)	**8 tsp.**	**40 mL**

Combine cornmeal and buttermilk in small bowl. Let stand for 15 minutes.

Combine next 5 ingredients in medium bowl. Make a well in centre.

Beat egg and canola oil with fork in small cup until frothy. Add to well. Add cornmeal mixture. Stir until just combined. Grease 8 muffin cups with cooking spray. Spoon about 1/4 cup (60 mL) batter into each cup.

Drop 1 tsp. (5 mL) jam into centre of each muffin. Divide and spoon remaining batter over jam. Pour about 1/4 inch (6 mm) water into empty muffin cups before baking muffins. Bake in 400°F (205°C) oven for about 15 minutes until golden and top springs back when pressed. Let stand in pan for 5 minutes before removing to wire rack to cool. Makes 8 muffins.

NUTRITION INFORMATION 1 muffin: 198 Calories; 4.9 g Total Fat (2.5 g Mono, 1.3 g Poly, 0.7 g Sat); 28 mg Cholesterol; 33 g Carbohydrate; 2 g Fibre; 5 g Protein; 257 mg Sodium

CHOICES 2 Starch; 1/2 Milk; 1 Fat & Oil

Breakfast Muffins

A simple breakfast muffin with the sweet taste of dates and apples. Great for a meal on the go or a lunch box snack.

All-purpose flour	**1 1/4 cups**	**300 mL**
Brown sugar, packed	**2/3 cup**	**150 mL**
Whole wheat flour	**1/2 cup**	**125 mL**
Bran flakes cereal	**1/3 cup**	**75 mL**
Baking powder	**1 tbsp.**	**15 mL**
Chopped pitted dates	**1 cup**	**250 mL**
Chopped dried apple	**1/2 cup**	**125 mL**
Large egg	**1**	**1**
Buttermilk (or reconstituted from powder)	**3/4 cup**	**175 mL**
Unsweetened applesauce	**1/3 cup**	**75 mL**
Finely grated orange zest	**1 tsp.**	**5 mL**

Combine first 5 ingredients in large bowl.

Add dates and apple. Mix well. Make a well in centre.

Beat egg with fork in small bowl. Add remaining 3 ingredients. Stir. Add to well. Stir until just moistened. Grease 12 muffin cups with cooking spray. Fill cups 3/4 full. Bake in 375°F (190°C) oven for about 20 minutes until wooden pick inserted in centre of muffin comes out clean. Let stand in pan for 5 minutes before removing to wire rack to cool. Makes 12 muffins.

NUTRITION INFORMATION 1 muffin: 188 Calories; 0.9 g Total Fat (0.2 g Mono, 0.2 g Poly, 0.3 g Sat); 19 mg Cholesterol; 44 g Carbohydrate; 3 g Fibre; 4 g Protein; 132 mg Sodium

CHOICES 1 Starch; 1 1/2 Fruit & Vegetable; 1 Sugar

Apple Gingerbread Mini-Muffins

A moist muffin with well-balanced flavours. Distinct spices add to the sweet apple and molasses flavours. The mini-muffins are great for a pop-in-your-mouth snack.

Diced, peeled apple (about 1 medium)	**1 cup**	**250 mL**
Lemon juice	**1 tsp.**	**5 mL**
All-purpose flour	**3/4 cup**	**175 mL**
Whole wheat flour	**3/4 cup**	**175 mL**
Brown sugar, packed	**1/4 cup**	**60 mL**
Ground ginger	**1 1/2 tsp.**	**7 mL**
Ground allspice	**1/4 tsp.**	**1 mL**
Large egg	**1**	**1**
Egg white (large)	**1**	**1**
Fancy (mild) molasses	**1/3 cup**	**75 mL**
Buttermilk (or reconstituted from powder)	**1/4 cup**	**60 mL**
Canola oil	**3 tbsp.**	**50 mL**
Baking soda	**3/4 tsp.**	**4 mL**

Combine apple and lemon juice in small bowl.

Combine next 5 ingredients in medium bowl. Make a well in centre. Add apple mixture to well. Do not stir.

Beat remaining 6 ingredients in same small bowl until combined. Add to apple mixture. Stir until just moistened. Spoon 1 rounded teaspoonful into each of 24 well-greased mini-muffin cups. Bake in 375°F (190°C) oven for about 10 minutes until wooden pick inserted in centre of muffin comes out clean. Let stand in pan for 2 minutes before removing to wire rack to cool. Makes 24 mini-muffins.

NUTRITION INFORMATION 1 mini-muffin: 74 Calories; 2.1 g Total Fat (1.1 g Mono, 0.6 g Poly, 0.2 g Sat); 9 mg Cholesterol; 13 g Carbohydrate; 1 g Fibre; 1 g Protein; 51 mg Sodium

CHOICES 1/2 Starch; 1/2 Fat & Oil; 1/2 Sugar

Pictured on page 144.

APPLE GINGERBREAD MUFFINS: Divide batter among 12 well-greased regular-sized muffin cups. Bake in 375°F (190°C) oven for about 20 minutes until wooden pick inserted in centre of muffin comes out clean. Let stand in pan for 5 minutes before removing to wire rack to cool. Makes 12 muffins.

Pumpkin And Fig Muffins

A moist, soft-crumb muffin with a delicate pumpkin flavour. The figs add a wonderful sweetness and nice texture.

All-purpose flour	1 cup	250 mL
Whole wheat flour	3/4 cup	175 mL
Dark brown sugar, packed	1/2 cup	125 mL
Baking powder	2 tbsp.	30 mL
Ground cinnamon	3/4 tsp.	4 mL
Ground nutmeg	1/2 tsp.	2 mL
Ground ginger	1/2 tsp.	2 mL
Milk	1 cup	250 mL
Canned pure pumpkin (no spices)	2/3 cup	150 mL
Canola oil	3 tbsp.	50 mL
Egg whites (large)	2	2
Chopped figs	1/2 cup	125 mL

Combine first 7 ingredients in large bowl. Make a well in centre.

Beat next 4 ingredients in medium bowl until smooth. Pour into well.

Add figs. Stir until just moistened. Grease 12 muffin cups with cooking spray. Fill cups 3/4 full. Bake in 400°F (205°C) oven for about 18 minutes until wooden pick inserted in centre of muffin comes out clean. Let stand in pan for 5 minutes before removing to wire rack to cool. Makes 12 muffins.

NUTRITION INFORMATION 1 muffin: 175 Calories; 4.1 g Total Fat (2.2 g Mono, 1.2 g Poly, 0.5 g Sat); 1 mg Cholesterol; 32 g Carbohydrate; 2 g Fibre; 4 g Protein; 211 mg Sodium

CHOICES 1 Starch; 1/2 Fruit & Vegetable; 1 Fat & Oil; 1 Sugar

Pepper Cheese Muffins

A savoury muffin speckled with red peppers, green basil and orange cheese. Red peppers may be roasted under the broiler, on the barbecue, or purchased in a jar and drained.

Canola oil	**1 tsp.**	**5 mL**
Chopped onion	**1 cup**	**250 mL**
Garlic clove, minced (or 1/4 tsp., 1 mL, powder)	**1**	**1**
All-purpose flour	**2 1/2 cups**	**625 mL**
Baking powder	**1 tbsp.**	**15 mL**
Chopped roasted red peppers (see Note)	**1 cup**	**250 mL**
Grated light sharp Cheddar cheese	**1/2 cup**	**125 mL**
Chopped fresh basil (or 1 1/2 tsp., 7 mL, dried)	**2 tbsp.**	**30 mL**
Chili paste (sambal oelek)	**1/2 tsp.**	**2 mL**
Pepper	**1/4 tsp.**	**1 mL**
Large egg	**1**	**1**
Milk	**1 cup**	**250 mL**
Canola oil	**1/3 cup**	**75 mL**

Heat first amount of canola oil in medium frying pan on medium. Add onion and garlic. Cook for 5 to 10 minutes, stirring often, until onion is soft and golden.

Combine flour and baking powder in large bowl.

Add onion mixture and next 5 ingredients. Stir. Make a well in centre.

Beat egg with fork in small bowl. Add milk and second amount of canola oil. Stir. Add to well. Stir until just moistened. Grease 12 muffin cups with cooking spray. Fill cups 3/4 full. Bake in 375°F (190°C) oven for 20 to 25 minutes until wooden pick inserted in centre of muffin comes out clean. Let stand in pan for 5 minutes before removing to wire rack to cool. Makes 12 muffins.

NUTRITION INFORMATION 1 muffin: 200 Calories; 8.7 g Total Fat (4.5 g Mono, 2.2 g Poly, 1.4 g Sat); 22 mg Cholesterol; 25 g Carbohydrate; 1 g Fibre; 6 g Protein; 142 mg Sodium

CHOICES 1 Starch; 1 Milk; 1 1/2 Fat & Oil

Pictured on page 143.

Note: Roasted peppers are available in jars at most grocery stores. Drain well.

Kid-Friendly Idea

Substitute 1 cup (250 mL) of your child's favourite cooked vegetables for the chili paste and red peppers.

Carrot Cheese Muffins

A sweet coconut and cream cheese filling bursts through the tops of these spiced carrot muffins.
Kids will love them for a snack or for breakfast.

All-purpose flour	3/4 cup	175 mL
Whole wheat flour	3/4 cup	175 mL
Brown sugar, packed	1/2 cup	125 mL
Baking powder	1 tsp.	5 mL
Baking soda	1 tsp.	5 mL
Ground cinnamon	1 tsp.	5 mL
Ground ginger	1/2 tsp.	2 mL
Salt	1/4 tsp.	1 mL
Ground nutmeg	1/8 tsp.	0.5 mL
Large egg	1	1
Light sour cream	3/4 cup	175 mL
Canola oil	3 tbsp.	50 mL
Finely shredded carrot	1 cup	250 mL
Chopped raisins	1/2 cup	125 mL
Vanilla	1 tsp.	5 mL
COCONUT CHEESE FILLING		
Light spreadable cream cheese	1/3 cup	75 mL
Flake coconut, toasted (see Tip, page 63)	1/4 cup	60 mL
Icing (confectioner's) sugar	2 tbsp.	30 mL
Vanilla	1/4 tsp.	1 mL

Combine first 9 ingredients in large bowl. Make a well in centre.

Beat egg, sour cream and canola oil in medium bowl. Stir in carrot, raisins and first amount of vanilla. Add to well. Stir until just moistened. Grease 12 muffin cups with cooking spray. Fill cups 3/4 full.

Coconut Cheese Filling: Combine all 4 ingredients in small bowl. Gently press 2 tsp. (10 mL) mixture down into centre of each muffin. Bake in 400°F (205°C) oven for about 15 minutes until golden. Let stand in pan for 5 minutes before removing to wire rack to cool. Makes 12 muffins.

NUTRITION INFORMATION 1 muffin: 188 Calories; 5.8 g Total Fat (2.9 g Mono, 1.3 g Poly, 2.2 g Sat); 21 mg Cholesterol; 32 g Carbohydrate; 2 g Fibre; 4 g Protein; 212 mg Sodium

CHOICES 1 Starch; 1/2 Fruit & Vegetable; 1 Fat & Oil; 1 Sugar

Pictured on page 144.

Date And Orange Loaf

This perfectly risen loaf has a great appearance and texture once sliced. The orange zest creates a wonderful complementary flavour to the dates. Delicious!

All-purpose flour	2 1/2 cups	625 mL
Granulated sugar	3/4 cup	175 mL
Baking powder	1 1/2 tbsp.	25 mL
Hard margarine (or butter)	1/3 cup	75 mL
Milk	1 cup	250 mL
Large eggs, fork-beaten	2	2
Finely grated orange zest	1 1/2 tsp.	7 mL
Chopped pitted dates	1 cup	250 mL

Combine flour, sugar and baking powder in large bowl. Make a well in centre.

Melt margarine in small saucepan on medium. Remove from heat. Stir in milk. Add eggs and zest. Stir. Add to well.

Add dates. Stir until combined. Turn into greased 9 x 5 x 3 inch (22 x 12.5 x 7.5 cm) loaf pan. Bake in 350°F (175ºC) oven for 55 to 60 minutes until wooden pick inserted in centre comes out clean. Let stand in pan for 10 minutes before removing to wire rack to cool. Cuts into 16 slices.

NUTRITION INFORMATION 1 slice: 199 Calories; 5.1 g Total Fat (2.9 g Mono, 0.6 g Poly, 1.2 g Sat); 28 mg Cholesterol; 36 g Carbohydrate; 2 g Fibre; 4 g Protein; 168 mg Sodium

CHOICES 1 Starch; 1 Fruit & Vegetable; 1 Fat & Oil; 1 Sugar

Pictured on page 144.

Pumpkin Bread

Moist, pumpkin-flavoured squares with a subtle hint of orange.

Granulated sugar	1/3 cup	75 mL
Hard margarine (or butter), softened	1/4 cup	60 mL
Can of pure pumpkin (no spices)	14 oz.	398 mL
Large eggs	2	2
Egg white (large)	1	1
Finely grated orange zest	2 tsp.	10 mL
All-purpose flour	1 1/4 cups	300 mL
Chopped pecans, toasted (see Tip, page 63)	1/3 cup	75 mL
Baking powder	4 tsp.	20 mL
Ground cinnamon	1/2 tsp.	2 mL
Ground nutmeg	1/4 tsp.	1 mL
Salt	1/4 tsp.	1 mL

Beat sugar and margarine in large bowl until light and creamy.

Add next 4 ingredients. Beat until well combined.

Combine remaining 6 ingredients in medium bowl. Add to pumpkin mixture. Stir. Turn into greased 8 x 8 inch (20 x 20 cm) pan. Bake in 350°F (175°C) oven for about 45 minutes until wooden pick inserted in centre comes out clean. Let stand in pan for 10 minutes before removing to wire rack to cool. Cuts into 16 pieces.

NUTRITION INFORMATION 1 piece: 119 Calories; 5.6 g Total Fat (3.3 g Mono, 0.9 g Poly, 1 g Sat); 27 mg Cholesterol; 15 g Carbohydrate; 1 g Fibre; 3 g Protein; 178 mg Sodium

CHOICES 1/2 Starch; 1/2 Fruit & Vegetable; 1 Fat & Oil

Kid-Friendly Idea

Omit pecans.

NUTRITION INFORMATION 1 piece (without nuts): 102 Calories; 3.9 g Total Fat (2.2 g Mono, 0.4 g Poly, 0.9 g Sat); 27 mg Cholesterol; 15 g Carbohydrate; 1 g Fibre; 2 g Protein; 178 mg Sodium

CHOICES 1/2 Starch; 1/2 Fruit & Vegetable; 1/2 Fat & Oil

Peanut Butter Cookies

Golden morsels with a classic peanut butter cookie appearance. This immensely satisfying snack has a mild peanut butter flavour.

Light smooth peanut butter	1/2 cup	125 mL
Brown sugar, packed	1/3 cup	75 mL
Hard margarine (or butter), softened	1/4 cup	60 mL
Large egg	1	1
Milk	1/4 cup	60 mL
Vanilla	1/2 tsp.	2 mL
All-purpose flour	1 1/2 cups	375 mL
Baking powder	1/2 tsp.	2 mL
Baking soda	1/2 tsp.	2 mL

Beat peanut butter, brown sugar and margarine in small bowl until light and creamy.

Add egg, milk and vanilla. Beat until well combined.

Combine flour, baking powder and baking soda in medium bowl. Add to margarine mixture. Mix well. Drop by slightly rounded tablespoonfuls, about 2 inches (5 cm) apart, onto greased baking sheet. Press with fork to flatten slightly. Bake in 375°F (190ºC) oven for about 12 minutes until lightly golden. Let stand on baking sheet for 10 minutes before removing to wire rack to cool. Makes about 30 cookies.

NUTRITION INFORMATION 1 cookie: 79 Calories; 4.2 g Total Fat (2.2 g Mono, 0.8 g Poly, 0.9 g Sat); 7 mg Cholesterol; 9 g Carbohydrate; trace Fibre; 2 g Protein; 72 mg Sodium

CHOICES 1/2 Starch; 1 Fat & Oil

Pictured on page 144.

Tropical Popsicles

The complementary flavours of banana and citrus fruits combine in these oh-so-refreshing popsicles. A delicious treat to enjoy on a summer day.

Can of crushed pineapple	14 oz.	398 mL
Mashed banana (about 2 medium)	1 cup	250 mL
Orange juice	1 cup	250 mL
Lime (or lemon) juice	1 tbsp.	15 mL
Plastic cups (5 oz., 142 mL, size)	14	14
Popsicle sticks	14	14

(continued on next page)

Combine first 4 ingredients in large bowl. Pour into 9 x 9 inch (22 x 22 cm) pan lined with plastic wrap. Freeze for about 1 hour until almost set. Process mixture in blender or food processor until smooth and creamy.

Divide and spoon mixture into cups. Insert popsicle stick into centre of each. Freeze for about 6 hours until firm. Dip cups into warm water briefly before turning out. Makes 14 popsicles.

NUTRITION INFORMATION 1 popsicle: 42 Calories; 0.1 g Total Fat (0 g Mono, 0 g Poly, 0 g Sat); 0 mg Cholesterol; 11 g Carbohydrate; 1 g Fibre; 0 g Protein; 1 mg Sodium

CHOICES 1 Fruit & Vegetable

Chewy Banana Nuggets

Soft, moist bites with a natural banana sweetness and a toasted coconut flavour. A healthy combination of ingredients that is great as a snack or as a light dessert.

Medium bananas	**3**	**3**
Lemon juice	**1 tbsp.**	**15 mL**
Medium unsweetened coconut	**1 1/2 cups**	**375 mL**
Finely chopped pitted dates	**1 cup**	**250 mL**
Quick-cooking rolled oats (not instant)	**1/2 cup**	**125 mL**
Vanilla	**1 tsp.**	**5 mL**
Ground cinnamon	**1/2 tsp.**	**2 mL**

Mash bananas and lemon juice in large bowl until smooth.

Add remaining 5 ingredients. Stir until moistened. Drop by 2 tsp. (10 mL) portions onto greased baking sheet. Bake on rack just above centre in 325°F (160°C) oven for about 30 minutes until dry and golden. Makes about 60 nuggets.

NUTRITION INFORMATION 1 nugget: 33 Calories; 1.6 g Total Fat (0.1 g Mono, 0 g Poly, 1.4 g Sat); 0 mg Cholesterol; 5 g Carbohydrate; 1 g Fibre; 0 g Protein; 1 mg Sodium

CHOICES 1/2 Fruit & Vegetable; 1/2 Fat & Oil

Popsicles can be made in popsicle molds or small waxed cups.

Fruity Granola Bars

Toasted oatmeal and coconut give a nutty flavour to these soft, fruity snack bars. Great for snacks or as a nutritious breakfast food. Kids will love them.

Quick-cooking rolled oats (not instant)	5 cups	1.25 L
Flake coconut	3/4 cup	175 mL
Can of low-fat sweetened condensed milk	11 oz.	300 mL
Unsweetened applesauce	2/3 cup	150 mL
Tub margarine, melted	1/4 cup	60 mL
Canola oil	1/4 cup	60 mL
Liquid honey	1/4 cup	60 mL
Dried cranberries	1 cup	250 mL
Finely chopped dried apricots	1 cup	250 mL

Combine rolled oats and coconut in medium bowl. Spread on ungreased baking sheet. Bake in 350°F (175°C) oven for 15 to 20 minutes, stirring every 5 minutes, until fragrant and coconut is golden.

Mix next 5 ingredients in large bowl until well combined. Add rolled oats mixture. Stir until moistened.

Add cranberries and apricots. Stir until well distributed. Line 9 x 13 inch (22 x 33 cm) pan with foil, leaving 1 inch (2.5 cm) overhang on long sides. Spray well with cooking spray. Transfer oat mixture to pan. Pack down firmly. Bake in 325°F (160°C) oven for about 45 minutes until set and golden. Cool completely. Using foil overhang, lift mixture from pan. Carefully peel off and discard foil. Cut mixture lengthwise into thirds. Cut each third into ten 1 1/4 inch (3 cm) wide bars. Wipe blade of sharp knife or run under hot water between each cut. Wrap bars individually in plastic wrap. Store at room temperature or place bars in resealable freezer bag to freeze for longer storage. Makes 30 bars.

NUTRITION INFORMATION 1 bar: 188 Calories; 7.5 g Total Fat (2.9 g Mono, 1.4 g Poly, 2.7 g Sat); 4 mg Cholesterol; 28 g Carbohydrate; 3 g Fibre; 4 g Protein; 40 mg Sodium

CHOICES 1 Starch; 1 Fruit & Vegetable; 1 1/2 Fat & Oil

Pictured on page 144.

Chilled Oatmeal Bars

Delicious, nutty granola bars with a variety of healthy ingredients. A substantial snack that is perfect for eating on the go.

Light smooth peanut butter	**1/2 cup**	**125 mL**
Hard margarine (or butter), softened	**2 tbsp.**	**30 mL**
Liquid honey	**2 tbsp.**	**30 mL**
Large eggs, fork-beaten	**2**	**2**
Vanilla	**1 tsp.**	**5 mL**
Quick-cooking rolled oats (not instant)	**2 cups**	**500 mL**
Sliced blanched almonds (with brown skin)	**1/2 cup**	**125 mL**
Unsalted shelled sunflower seeds	**1/4 cup**	**60 mL**
Unsalted shelled pumpkin seeds	**1/4 cup**	**60 mL**

Combine peanut butter, margarine and honey in large saucepan. Heat and stir on medium until smooth. Remove from heat.

Add eggs and vanilla. Beat with fork or whisk until slightly thickened.

Add remaining 4 ingredients. Stir until coated. Line 9 x 9 inch (22 x 22 cm) pan with foil, leaving 1 inch (2.5 cm) overhang on 2 sides. Transfer oat mixture to pan. Pack down firmly. Chill for about 4 hours until firm. Using foil overhang, lift mixture from pan. Carefully peel off foil and discard. Cuts into 36 bars.

NUTRITION INFORMATION 1 bar: 77 Calories; 4.6 g Total Fat (2 g Mono, 1.5 g Poly, 0.7 g Sat); 12 mg Cholesterol; 7 g Carbohydrate; 1 g Fibre; 3 g Protein; 31 mg Sodium

CHOICES 1/2 Starch; 1 Fat & Oil

Variation: After packing down oat mixture in pan lined with greased foil, bake in 350°F (175°) oven for about 20 minutes until golden. Let stand on wire rack until cool.

Cut and wrap individual bars in plastic wrap. Keep a supply in the refrigerator and the freezer for a ready-made "snack bar." Great for bag lunches or after-school snacks.

Pizza Swirls

These whole wheat pinwheels make a great snack. Wrap swirls individually in plastic wrap for a take-along snack. Good warm or cold.

All-purpose flour	1 cup	250 mL
Whole wheat flour	1 cup	250 mL
Baking powder	1 tbsp.	15 mL
Dried basil	1/2 tsp.	2 mL
Dried oregano	1/4 tsp.	1 mL
Salt	1/4 tsp.	1 mL
Skim (or 1%) milk	1/2 cup	125 mL
Olive (or canola) oil	1/3 cup	75 mL
Garlic (or regular) chili sauce (optional)	1 tsp.	5 mL
Yellow cornmeal	1 tbsp.	15 mL
Pizza sauce	1/2 cup	125 mL
Diced red or yellow pepper	1/2 cup	125 mL
Fat-free cooked ham slices, diced (about 1 cup, 250 mL)	4	4
Grated part-skim mozzarella cheese	1 cup	250 mL
Finely grated fresh Parmesan cheese	2 tbsp.	30 mL

Combine first 6 ingredients in large bowl. Make a well in centre.

Pour milk, olive oil and chili sauce into well. Stir until ball starts to form. Turn out onto lightly floured surface. Knead 8 times.

Spread cornmeal across 10 x 20 inch (25 x 50 cm) work surface. Roll out dough over cornmeal to 8 x 18 inch (20 x 46 cm) rectangle.

Spread pizza sauce over dough, leaving 1/4 inch (6 mm) border around edge.

Combine remaining 4 ingredients in medium bowl. Scatter evenly over pizza sauce. Roll up, jelly roll-style, from long side. Dough will be somewhat stiff. Pinch edge against roll to seal, leaving ends open. Slice into twenty 1 inch (2.5 cm) thick rounds. Arrange, cut-side down, about 1 inch (2.5 cm) apart on greased baking sheet. Bake in 425°F (220ºC) oven for about 10 minutes until starting to turn golden. Let stand on baking sheet for 5 minutes before removing to wire rack to cool. Makes 20 swirls.

NUTRITION INFORMATION 1 swirl: 120 Calories; 5.9 g Total Fat (3.5 g Mono, 0.6 g Poly, 1.5 g Sat); 8 mg Cholesterol; 12 g Carbohydrate; 1 g Fibre; 5 g Protein; 264 mg Sodium

CHOICES 1/2 Starch; 1/2 Milk; 1/2 Protein; 1/2 Fat & Oil

Parmesan Chicken Fingers

These flavourful fingers are ready in about 30 minutes. May be frozen after cooking and reheated in the microwave or oven. They're even good cold—one batch will go a long way for snacking!

Boneless, skinless chicken breast halves	**1 lb.**	**454 g**
Non-fat plain yogurt (or fat-free sour cream)	**1/2 cup**	**125 mL**
Garlic and herb no-salt seasoning (such as Mrs. Dash)	**1 tsp.**	**5 mL**
Paprika	**1/2 tsp.**	**2 mL**
Garlic powder (optional)	**1/4 tsp.**	**1 mL**
Lemon pepper	**1/4 tsp.**	**1 mL**
Finely grated fresh Parmesan cheese	**2/3 cup**	**150 mL**
Fine dry bread crumbs	**2/3 cup**	**150 mL**
Chopped fresh parsley (or 1/2 tsp., 2 mL, flakes), optional	**2 tsp.**	**10 mL**

Cut each chicken breast lengthwise into 6 or 7 strips.

Combine next 5 ingredients in medium bowl. Add chicken. Stir until coated. Cover. Marinate in refrigerator for at least 1 hour.

Combine cheese, breadcrumbs and parsley in shallow dish. Remove chicken strips from marinade, 1 at a time, making sure to leave some yogurt mixture on each. Press both sides of strips into cheese mixture until coated. Arrange in single layer on well-greased baking sheet. Spray chicken with cooking spray. Bake in 425°F (220ºC) oven for 15 to 20 minutes until no longer pink inside. Serve hot or cold. Serves 8.

NUTRITION INFORMATION 1 serving: 150 Calories; 4.2 g Total Fat (1.2 g Mono, 0.4 g Poly, 2.1 g Sat); 40 mg Cholesterol; 9 g Carbohydrate; trace Fibre; 18 g Protein; 258 mg Sodium

CHOICES 1/2 Starch; 2 1/2 Protein

Pictured on page 143.

Corn Yogurt Dip

The creamy cheese and sweet corn flavours in this dip will appeal to children and adults alike. Serve warm with fresh, crisp veggies, such as carrot sticks, cucumber pieces, celery sticks, radishes or cauliflower florets.

Corn relish	**1/2 cup**	**125 mL**
Low-fat plain yogurt	**1/2 cup**	**125 mL**
Grated light sharp Cheddar cheese	**1/3 cup**	**75 mL**
Chopped fresh chives	**2 tbsp.**	**30 mL**

Combine all 4 ingredients in small saucepan. Heat and stir on medium for 5 to 6 minutes until cheese is melted. Makes 1 cup (250 mL).

NUTRITION INFORMATION 2 tbsp. (30 mL): 40 Calories; 1.3 g Total Fat (0.4 g Mono, 0.1 g Poly, 0.8 g Sat); 4 mg Cholesterol; 5 g Carbohydrate; trace Fibre; 2 g Protein; 130 mg Sodium

CHOICES 1/2 Fruit & Vegetable; 1/2 Protein

Pictured on page 143.

1. Pepper Cheese Muffins, page 132
2. Chicken Samosas, page 146
3. Corn Yogurt Dip, this page
4. Parmesan Chicken Fingers, page 141
5. Pesto Cheese Spirals, page 149

Ham And Melon Skewers

Perfectly woven flavours on a refreshing summer kabob.

Small cantaloupe	1	1
Fat-free cooked ham slices	4	4
Bamboo skewers (4 inch, 10 cm, length), or cocktail picks	12	12

Cut cantaloupe in half. Scoop out and discard seeds and pulp. Cut each half into 6 wedges. Cut off and discard rind. Cut each wedge crosswise into 3 pieces, for a total of 36 pieces.

Cut each ham slice lengthwise into 3 strips.

Thread 3 cantaloupe pieces alternately with 1 ham strip onto each skewer. Repeat with remaining cantaloupe, ham and skewers. Makes 12 skewers.

NUTRITION INFORMATION   1 skewer: 31 Calories; 0.7 g Total Fat (0.3 g Mono, 0.1 g Poly, 0.2 g Sat); 6 mg Cholesterol; 4 g Carbohydrate; trace Fibre; 3 g Protein; 173 mg Sodium

CHOICES   1/2 Fruit & Vegetable; 1/2 Protein

1. Date And Orange Loaf, page 134
2. Piñana Milk Smoothie, page 124
3. Strawberry Orange Smoothie, page 127
4. Peanut Butter Cookies, page 136
5. Apple Gingerbread Mini-Muffins, page 130
6. Fruity Granola Bars, page 138
7. Carrot Cheese Muffins, page 133

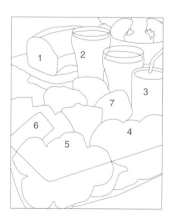

Chicken Samosas

Pronounced sah-MOH-sahs, these crisp pastries are filled with tender chicken and cooked vegetables. Good as is or dipped in sweet chili sauce, chutney, plum sauce or ketchup.

CHICKEN FILLING

Olive (or canola) oil	1 tbsp.	15 mL
Finely chopped onion	2 cups	500 mL
Lean ground chicken	1 lb.	454 g
Lemon pepper (optional)	1/2 tsp.	2 mL
Garlic cloves, minced (or 1/2 tsp., 2 mL, powder)	2	2
Potatoes (about 2 small), peeled and diced	1/4 lb.	113 g
Frozen peas	2/3 cup	150 mL
Low-sodium prepared chicken broth	1/2 cup	125 mL
Grated carrot	1/3 cup	75 mL
Garlic and herb no-salt seasoning (such as Mrs. Dash)	1 1/2 tsp.	7 mL
All-purpose flour	2 tbsp.	30 mL
Water	3 tbsp.	50 mL
Samosa wrappers (found in freezer section of large grocery stores or East Indian markets)	18	18

Chicken Filling: Heat olive oil in large saucepan on medium. Add onion. Cook for 5 to 10 minutes, stirring often, until onion is soft and golden.

Add ground chicken, lemon pepper and garlic. Cook on medium for about 5 minutes, stirring constantly, until chicken is broken up and no pink remains.

Add next 5 ingredients. Stir. Bring to a boil. Reduce heat to medium. Cover. Cook for 15 to 20 minutes, stirring occasionally, until potato is tender. Remove cover. Increase heat if necessary to boil off any remaining moisture. Cool. Makes 3 1/2 cups (875 mL) filling.

Stir flour into water in small cup until consistency of smooth paste.

1. Lay 1 samosa wrapper on work surface. **2– 6.** Fold according to diagram, moistening edges of wrapper with flour mixture. Turn over. Spoon 3 tbsp. (50 mL) chicken filling into pocket. **7.** Moisten flaps with flour mixture. Fold to seal. Arrange, seam-side down, on greased baking sheet. Repeat with remaining wrappers, flour mixture and filling. Spray samosas lightly with cooking spray. Bake in 400°F (205ºC) oven for about 15 minutes until crisp and lightly golden. Makes 18 samosas.

(continued on next page)

NUTRITION INFORMATION 1 samosa: 176 Calories; 4.7 g Total Fat (0.6 g Mono, 0.3 g Poly, 0.2 g Sat); 3 mg Cholesterol; 24 g Carbohydrate; 1 g Fibre; 9 g Protein; 225 mg Sodium

CHOICES 1 1/2 Starch; 1 Protein

Pictured on page 143.

To Make Ahead: Prepare to baking stage. Wrap. Freeze. Bake in 400°F (205°C) oven for about 15 minutes until crisp and lightly golden. Or bake first. Wrap. Freeze. Reheat in microwave.

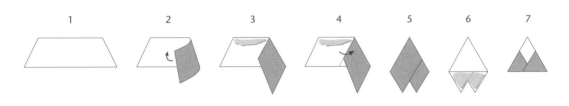

Cheese Tortillas

Crisp tortillas with a spicy cheese topping. Best served warm.

Light spreadable cream cheese	1/2 cup	125 mL
Chili sauce	1 tbsp.	15 mL
Low-sodium soy sauce	1 tbsp.	15 mL
Whole wheat flour tortillas (10 inch, 25 cm, diameter)	2	2
Sesame seeds	2 tsp.	10 mL

Combine cream cheese, chili sauce and soy sauce in small bowl.

Place tortillas on ungreased baking sheet. Divide and spread cream cheese mixture on 1 side of each tortilla.

Sprinkle with sesame seeds. Bake in 425°F (220°C) oven for about 10 minutes until tortillas are crisp. Cut each into 8 wedges. Makes 16 wedges.

NUTRITION INFORMATION 2 wedges: 76 Calories; 4.1 g Total Fat (1.4 g Mono, 0.6 g Poly, 1.9 g Sat); 10 mg Cholesterol; 7 g Carbohydrate; 2 g Fibre; 3 g Protein; 248 mg Sodium

CHOICES 1/2 Starch; 1 Fat & Oil

Cheesy Pocket Puffs

These attractive, golden crescents have a warm, cheese filling. Great with Corn Yogurt Dip, page 142.

Whole wheat flour	1 cup	250 mL
All-purpose flour	1 cup	250 mL
Instant yeast	2 tsp.	10 mL
Salt	1/4 tsp.	1 mL
Very warm water	3/4 cup	175 mL
Olive (or canola) oil	1 tbsp.	15 mL
Granulated sugar	1 tsp.	5 mL
CHEESY FILLING		
Mashed non-fat creamed cottage cheese	2/3 cup	150 mL
Crumbled low-fat feta cheese (about 3 oz., 85 g)	2/3 cup	150 mL
Finely chopped green onion	1 tbsp.	15 mL
Finely chopped fresh dill (or 1/4 tsp., 1 mL, dill weed)	1 tsp.	5 mL
Garlic powder (optional)	1/8 tsp.	0.5 mL
Pepper, sprinkle		
Sesame seeds	1 tsp.	15 mL

Put first 4 ingredients into food processor fitted with dough blade.

Stir water, olive oil and sugar in liquid measure until sugar is dissolved. With motor running, pour mixture through feed chute. Process for 30 to 40 seconds until dough comes together and ball begins to form. Place dough in greased bowl, turning once to grease top. Cover with greased waxed paper and tea towel. Let stand in oven with light on and door closed for about 30 minutes until starting to rise.

Cheesy Filling: Mix first 6 ingredients in small bowl until creamy. Makes 1 cup (250 mL) filling.

Punch dough down. Divide into 8 portions. Lightly grease work surface with cooking spray. Roll out 1 portion of dough to 3 1/2 inch (9 cm) circle. Cover remaining portions to keep from drying out. Place about 2 tbsp. (30 mL) filling on 1/2 of circle. Dampen edge of circle with water. Fold dough over. Pinch edges together to seal. Place on lightly greased baking sheet. Repeat with remaining portions of dough and filling. Lightly spray surface of puffs with cooking spray. Sprinkle with sesame seeds. Cover with tea towel. Let stand in oven with light on and door closed for about 1 hour until doubled in size. Bake in 375°F (190°C) oven for about 15 minutes until golden. Remove to wire rack to cool. Makes 8 puffs.

NUTRITION INFORMATION 1 puff: 190 Calories; 5.2 g Total Fat (2.1 g Mono, 0.5 g Poly, 2.3 g Sat); 6 mg Cholesterol; 26 g Carbohydrate; 3 g Fibre; 11 g Protein; 162 mg Sodium

CHOICES 1 1/2 Starch; 1 Protein; 1/2 Fat & Oil

Pesto Cheese Spirals

Scrumptious! These easy, fluffy biscuits are spiralled with basil pesto. Freeze in a sealed container and enjoy them thawed to room temperature, or reheat from frozen by covering with foil and baking in 450°F (230ºC) oven for 15 to 20 minutes until warmed.

All-purpose flour	2 1/4 cups	550 mL
Baking powder	1 tbsp.	15 mL
Granulated sugar	1 tbsp.	15 mL
Hard margarine (or butter)	1 tbsp.	15 mL
Buttermilk (or reconstituted from powder), approximately	1 cup	250 mL
Basil pesto	1/3 cup	75 mL
Crumbled low-fat feta cheese (about 2 1/2 oz., 70 g)	1/2 cup	125 mL

Combine flour, baking powder and sugar in large bowl. Cut in margarine until consistency of coarse crumbs.

Stir in enough buttermilk to make soft, sticky dough. Turn out onto lightly floured surface. Knead about 8 times until smooth. Roll out dough to 6 × 12 inch (15 × 30 cm) rectangle.

Spread pesto on dough. Sprinkle with cheese. Roll up, jelly roll-style, from long side. Pinch edge against roll to seal. Cut into 12 slices, about 1 inch (2.5 cm) thick. Arrange, cut-side down, about 2 inches (5 cm) apart, on greased baking sheet. Bake in 475°F (240ºC) oven for about 15 minutes until edges are lightly browned. Let stand on baking sheet for 5 minutes before removing to wire rack to cool. Makes 12 spirals.

NUTRITION INFORMATION 1 spiral: 151 Calories; 3.5 g Total Fat (2.6 g Mono, 0.4 g Poly, 1.6 g Sat); 4 mg Cholesterol; 18 g Carbohydrate; 1 g Fibre; 4 g Protein; 152 mg Sodium

CHOICES 1 Starch; 1/2 Milk; 1/2 Fat & Oil

Pictured on page 143.

Measurement Tables

Throughout this book measurements are given in Conventional and Metric measure. To compensate for differences between the two measurements due to rounding, a full metric measure is not always used. The cup used is the standard 8 fluid ounce. Temperature is given in degrees Fahrenheit and Celsius. Baking pan measurements are in inches and centimetres as well as quarts and litres. An exact metric conversion is given below as well as the working equivalent (Standard Measure).

OVEN TEMPERATURES

Fahrenheit (°F)	Celsius (°C)
175°	80°
200°	95°
225°	110°
250°	120°
275°	140°
300°	150°
325°	160°
350°	175°
375°	190°
400°	205°
425°	220°
450°	230°
475°	240°
500°	260°

SPOONS

Conventional Measure	Metric Exact Conversion Millilitre (mL)	Metric Standard Measure Millilitre (mL)
$1/8$ teaspoon (tsp.)	0.6 mL	0.5 mL
$1/4$ teaspoon (tsp.)	1.2 mL	1 mL
$1/2$ teaspoon (tsp.)	2.4 mL	2 mL
1 teaspoon (tsp.)	4.7 mL	5 mL
2 teaspoons (tsp.)	9.4 mL	10 mL
1 tablespoon (tbsp.)	14.2 mL	15 mL

CUPS

Conventional Measure	Metric Exact Conversion Millilitre (mL)	Metric Standard Measure Millilitre (mL)
$1/4$ cup (4 tbsp.)	56.8 mL	60 mL
$1/3$ cup ($5^{1}/3$ tbsp.)	75.6 mL	75 mL
$1/2$ cup (8 tbsp.)	113.7 mL	125 mL
$2/3$ cup ($10^{2}/3$ tbsp.)	151.2 mL	150 mL
$3/4$ cup (12 tbsp.)	170.5 mL	175 mL
1 cup (16 tbsp.)	227.3 mL	250 mL
$4^{1}/2$ cups	1022.9 mL	1000 mL (1 L)

PANS

Conventional Inches	Metric Centimetres
8x8 inch	20x20 cm
9x9 inch	22x22 cm
9x13 inch	22x33 cm
10x15 inch	25x38 cm
11x17 inch	28x43 cm
8x2 inch round	20x5 cm
9x2 inch round	22x5 cm
$10x4^{1}/2$ inch tube	25x11 cm
8x4x3 inch loaf	20x10x7.5 cm
9x5x3 inch loaf	22x12.5x7.5 cm

DRY MEASUREMENTS

Conventional Measure Ounces (oz.)	Metric Exact Conversion Grams (g)	Metric Standard Measure Grams (g)
1 oz.	28.3 g	28 g
2 oz.	56.7 g	57 g
3 oz.	85.0 g	85 g
4 oz.	113.4 g	125 g
5 oz.	141.7 g	140 g
6 oz.	170.1 g	170 g
7 oz.	198.4 g	200 g
8 oz.	226.8 g	250 g
16 oz.	453.6 g	500 g
32 oz.	907.2 g	1000 g (1 kg)

CASSEROLES (Canada & Britain)

Standard Size Casserole	Exact Metric Measure
1 qt. (5 cups)	1.13 L
$1^{1}/2$ qts. ($7^{1}/2$ cups)	1.69 L
2 qts. (10 cups)	2.25 L
$2^{1}/2$ qts. ($12^{1}/2$ cups)	2.81 L
3 qts. (15 cups)	3.38 L
4 qts. (20 cups)	4.5 L
5 qts. (25 cups)	5.63 L

CASSEROLES (United States)

Standard Size Casserole	Exact Metric Measure
1 qt. (4 cups)	900 mL
$1^{1}/2$ qts. (6 cups)	1.35 L
2 qts. (8 cups)	1.8 L
$2^{1}/2$ qts. (10 cups)	2.25 L
3 qts. (12 cups)	2.7 L
4 qts. (16 cups)	3.6 L
5 qts. (20 cups)	4.5 L

Tip Index

C

Cardamom – to bruise 23
Coconut – to toast 63

J

Jalapeño peppers – to cut 113

M

Meatballs – to form 25
Microwave – to cook evenly 49

N

Nuts – to toast 63

P

Popsicles – to make 137

S

Seeds – to toast 63
Snacks – to store 139
Squares – to pre-cut 139

T

Toasting coconut, nuts and seeds 63
Tomato paste – to store 43
Tortillas – to warm 15

Recipe Index

A

Apple Cranberry Chutney 117
Apple Curry Wraps 12
Apple Gingerbread Mini-Muffins 130
Apple Gingerbread Muffins 130
Apple Topping 122
Apples, Buttermilk Pancakes And 122
Apricot Beef Casserole 58
Apricot Clafouti 118
Apricot-Glazed Chicken 70
Apricot Purée 70
Artichoke And Ham Pie 40
Asian Rice Bowl 50
Asparagus
    Beef And 14
    Lemon Asparagus Penne 45
    Pesto Chicken Wraps 74
    Shrimp And Asparagus Stir-Fry 28
Asparagus And Mushrooms 109

B

Balsamic Tenderloin, Maple 34
Banana Nuggets, Chewy 137
Banana Shake, Peanut Butter 123

Barbecue/Grill
    Beef And Mandarin Salad 11
    Chili Turkey Burgers 20
    Grilled Chicken And Salsa 76
    Grilled Pork Sandwich 78
    Lemon Garlic Steaks 16
    Maple Balsamic Tenderloin 34
    Marinated Halibut Skewers 31
    Mushroom Beef Burgers 13
    Pepper Pork Skewers 38
    Spinach And Pork Salad 79
    Succulent Lamb Chops .37
Bars, Chilled Oatmeal 139
Bars, Fruity Granola 138
Basic Beef Stew 80
Beef
    Apple Curry Wraps 12
    Apricot Beef Casserole .58
    Basic Beef Stew 80
    Ground Beef Sauce 86
    Lemon Garlic Steaks 16
    Mushroom Beef Burgers 13
    Penne And Meat Sauce .86
    Potato Beef Pie 87
    Slow Cooker Fajitas 62

152

Spicy Beef Pie 81
Beef And Asparagus 14
Beef And Mandarin Salad 11
Beef And Rice Lettuce Wraps 77
Beef And Tomato Stew 57
Beef Filling 87
Beef In Red Wine 67
Beverages
　　Hawaiian Smoothie 124
　　Peanut Butter Banana Shake 123
　　Piñana Milk Smoothie 124
　　Strawberry Orange Smoothie 127
Biscuits, Buttermilk Tea 120
Blackened Snapper 27
Blueberry Cobbler 119
Bows And Fresh Vegetables 44
Bread, Pumpkin 135
Breakfast Muffins 129
Burgers, Chili Turkey 20
Burgers, Mushroom Beef .13
Buttermilk Pancakes and Apples 122
Buttermilk Tea Biscuits 120
Butternut Squash, Maple 104

C

Cacciatore, Chicken 48
Carrot Cheese Muffins 133
Cauliflower, Roasted 102
Cheese Muffins, Pepper .132
Cheese Roll, Spinach And 46
Cheese Sauce, Lightened-Up 114
Cheese Sauce, Parmesan .24
Cheese Spirals, Pesto 149
Cheese Supper, Pasta And 56
Cheese Tortillas 147
Cheesy Filling 148
Cheesy Pocket Puffs 148
Chewy Banana Nuggets .137
Chicken
　　Apricot-Glazed 70
　　Asian Rice Bowl 50
　　Creamy Chicken Spaghetti 84
　　Garden Chicken Stew 85
　　Grilled Chicken And Salsa 76
　　Moroccan 65
　　Orange 64

Oriental Citrus 21
Parmesan Chicken Fingers 141
Peanut Butter 61
Pesto Chicken Wraps 74
Pineapple Chicken Balls .19
Pineapple Chicken Skewers 68
Poached Spice 22
Chicken And Pea Risotto .26
Chicken Cacciatore 48
Chicken Filling 146
Chicken Mushroom Filling 24
Chicken Mushroom Rolls .24
Chicken Paprikash 59
Chicken Samosas 146
Chicken Stroganoff 51
Chicken Sauce 84
Chili Marinade, Lime 68
Chili Turkey Burgers 20
Chilled Oatmeal Bars 139
Chops, Succulent Lamb 37
Chutney, Apple Cranberry 117
Citrus Chicken, Oriental 21
Clafouti, Apricot 118
Cobbler, Blueberry 119
Cobbler, Fruit 119
Coconut Cheese Filling .133
Condiments
　　Apple Cranberry Chutney 117
　　Spicy Roasted Pepper Sauce 113
　　Tropical Yogurt Topping 116
Cookies, Peanut Butter .136
Cool Yogurt Sauce 27
Corn And Onion, Creamy 96
Corn Muffin Surprise 128
Corn Salsa, Fresh 76
Corn Yogurt Dip 142
Couscous, Easy 92
Couscous, Herb 22
Cranberry Chutney, Apple 117
Creamed Veggie Spaghetti 94
Creamy Chicken Spaghetti 84
Creamy Corn And Onion 96
Creamy Fish Stew 29
Creamy Mushroom Sauce 116
Creamy Spinach 106
Crispy Spiced Potatoes .100

Crumbed Fish, Parmesan 30
Crunchy Rice Salad 96
Curry Sauce, Turkey In 49
Curry Wraps, Apple 12

D

Date And Orange Loaf 134
Desserts
   Apricot Clafouti 118
   Blueberry Cobbler 119
   Buttermilk Pancakes And Apples 122
   Fruit Cobbler 119
   Pear And Yogurt Freeze 123
   Strawberry Shortcakes 120
   Tropical Trifles 121
Dill Halibut, Mustard 75
Dill Salmon, Mustard 75
Dip, Corn Yogurt 142
Dipping Sauce, Onion And Garlic 115
Dressing
   Lemon 79, 97
   Lime 97
   Mustard Mayonnaise 39
   Parmesan 11
   Yogurt And Herb 101

E

Easy Couscous 92

F

Fajitas, Slow Cooker 62
Fennel Bake, Potato And 102
Fig Muffins, Pumpkin And 131
Filling
   Beef 87
   Cheesy 148
   Chicken 146
   Chicken Mushroom 24
   Coconut Cheese 133
Fish & Seafood
   Blackened Snapper 27
   Creamy Fish Stew .29
   Marinated Halibut Skewers 31
   Mustard Dill Halibut 75
   Mustard Dill Salmon 75
   Mustard Honey Salmon 55

   Orange Teriyaki Fish 74
   Parmesan Crumbed Fish 30
   Shrimp And Asparagus Stir-Fry 28
Fish Parcels 32
Fluffy Garlic Potatoes 88
Fresh Corn Salsa 76
Fried Rice 98
Fruit Cobbler 119
Fruity Granola Bars 138

G

Garden Chicken Stew 85
Garlic Dipping Sauce, Onion And 115
Garlic Pork Supper, Roasted 82
Garlic Potatoes, Fluffy .88
Garlic Steaks, Lemon 16
Gingerbread Mini-Muffins, Apple 130
Gingerbread Muffins, Apple 130
Granola Bars, Fruity 138
Grill, see Barbecue
Grilled Chicken And Salsa 76
Grilled Pork Mushrooms 69
Grilled Pork Sandwich .78
Ground Beef Sauce 86

H

Halibut, Mustard Dill 75
Halibut Skewers, Marinated 31
Ham
   Artichoke And Ham Pie 40
   Fried Rice 98
   Pizza Swirls 140
Ham And Melon Skewers 145
Hawaiian Smoothie 124
Herb Couscous 22
Herb Dressing, Yogurt And 101
Herb Pasta, Tomato 95
Honey Salmon, Mustard 55

K

Kid-Friendly Ideas
   Apple Curry Wraps 13
   Asian Rice Bowl 51
   Basic Beef Stew 81
   Beef And Asparagus 15
   Beef And Tomato Stew 57

Beef In Red Wine 67
Blackened Snapper 27
Bows And Fresh Vegetables 45
Chicken Cacciatore 48
Chicken Mushroom Rolls 25
Creamed Veggie Spaghetti 95
Crispy Spiced Wedges 100
Easy Couscous 92
Fried Rice 98
Garden Chicken Stew 85
Grilled Chicken And Salsa 77
Lemon Garlic Steaks 16
Maple Butternut Squash 104
Marinated Halibut Skewers 31
Pea Medley 110
Pepper Cheese Muffins 132
Poached Spice Chicken 23
Pork And Pineapple Stir-Fry 33
Potato Salad 101
Pumpkin Bread 135
Roasted Garlic Pork Supper 82
Spicy Roasted Pepper Sauce 113
Spinach And Cheese Roll 47
Spinach And Pork Salad 79
Spinach Mushroom Rice 93
Stuffed Zucchini 41
Vegetable Lasagne 43
Warm Pork Salad 39
Zucchini Pepper Combo 105

L

Lamb
    Roasted Lamb Rack 52
    Peppered 73
    Succulent Lamb Chops 37
Lasagne, Vegetable 42
Lemon Asparagus Penne 45
Lemon Dressing 79, 97
Lemon Garlic Steaks 16
Lentil Soup, Squash And 63
Lettuce Wraps, Beef And Rice 77
Lightened-Up Cheese Sauce 114
Lime Chili Marinade 68
Lime Dressing 97
Loaf, Date And Orange 134

M

Mandarin Salad, Beef and 11
Maple Balsamic Tenderloin 34
Maple Butternut Squash 104
Marinade, Lime Chili 68
Marinade, Zesty 78
Marinated Halibut Skewers 31
Mashed Potato Topping 87
Mashed Sweet Potatoes 103
Mayonnaise, Mustard 39
Meat Sauce, Penne And 86
Melon Skewers, Ham And 145
Milk Smoothie, Piñana 124
Moroccan Chicken 65
Muffins
    Apple Gingerbread 130
    Apple Gingerbread, Mini 130
    Breakfast 129
    Carrot Cheese 133
    Corn Muffin Surprise 128
    Pepper Cheese Muffins 132
    Pumpkin And Fig 131
Mushroom Beef Burgers 13
Mushroom Polenta 99
Mushroom Rice, Spinach 93
Mushroom Rolls, Chicken 24
Mushroom Sauce, Creamy 116
Mushrooms, Asparagus And 109
Mushrooms, Grilled Pork 69
Mustard Dill Halibut 75
Mustard Dill Salmon 75
Mustard Honey Salmon 55
Mustard Mayonnaise 39

N

Noodles, Quick Pork With 83
Nuggets, Chewy Banana 137

O

Oatmeal Bars, Chilled 139
Onion And Garlic Dipping Sauce 115
Onion, Creamy Corn And 96
Orange Chicken 64
Orange Loaf, Date And 134
Orange Sauce 66

155

Orange Smoothie, Strawberry 127
Orange Teriyaki Fish 74
Oriental Citrus Chicken 21
Oven-Fried Vegetables 112

P

Pancakes And Apples, Buttermilk 122
Paprikash, Chicken 59
Parcels, Fish 32
Parmesan Cheese Sauce 24
Parmesan Chicken Fingers 141
Parmesan Crumbed Fish 30
Parmesan Dressing 11
Pasta
    Bows And Fresh Vegetables 44
    Chicken Mushroom Rolls 24
    Chicken Paprikash 59
    Creamed Veggie Spaghetti 94
    Creamy Chicken Spaghetti 84
    Lemon Asparagus Penne 45
    Penne And Meat Sauce 86
    Quick Pork With Noodles 83
    Tomato Herb 95
    Vegetable Lasagne 42
Pasta And Cheese Supper 56
Pasta Salad 97
Pea Medley 110
Pea Risotto, Chicken And 26
Peanut Butter Banana Shake 123
Peanut Butter Chicken 61
Peanut Butter Cookies 136
Pear And Yogurt Freeze 123
Penne And Meat Sauce 86
Penne, Lemon Asparagus 45
Pepper Cheese Muffins 132
Pepper Combo, Zucchini 105
Pepper Pizza, Roasted Red 47
Pepper Pork Skewers 38
Pepper Sauce, Roasted 46
Pepper Sauce, Spicy Roasted 113
Peppered Lamb 73
Pesto Cheese Spirals 149
Pesto Chicken Wraps 74
Pie, Savoury
    Artichoke And Ham 40
    Potato Beef 87

Spicy Beef 81
Piñana Milk Smoothie 124
Pineapple Chicken Balls 19
Pineapple Chicken Skewers 68
Pineapple Stir-Fry, Pork And 33
Pizza Swirls 140
Pizza, Roasted Red Pepper 47
Poached Spice Chicken 22
Polenta, Mushroom 99
Popsicles, Tropical 136
Pork
    Artichoke And Ham Pie 40
    Fried Rice 98
    Grilled Pork Mushrooms 69
    Grilled Pork Sandwich 78
    Ham And Melon Skewers 145
    Maple Balsamic Tenderloin 34
    Pepper Pork Skewers 38
    Pizza Swirls 140
    Quick Pork With Noodles 83
    Roasted Garlic Pork Supper 82
    Spinach And Pork Salad 79
    Warm Pork Salad 39
Pork And Pineapple Stir-Fry 33
Pork With Orange Sauce 66
Potato And Fennel Bake 102
Potato Beef Pie 87
Potato Salad 101
Potatoes
    Fluffy Garlic 88
    Mashed Potato Topping 87
    Mashed Sweet 103
    Spicy Crispy 100
    Warm Potato Salad 91
Puffs, Cheesy Pocket 148
Pumpkin And Fig Muffins 131
Pumpkin Bread 135
Purée, Apricot 70

Q

Quick Pork With Noodles 83

R

Rack, Roasted Lamb 52
Red Pepper Pizza, Roasted 47
Red Wine, Beef In 67

Rice
    Asian Rice Bowl 50
    Beef And Rice Lettuce Wraps 77
    Chicken And Pea Risotto .26
    Crunchy Rice Salad 96
    Fried 98
    Spinach Mushroom 93
    Turkey In Curry Sauce 49
Risotto, Chicken And Pea 26
Roast Supreme, Turkey 60
Roasted Cauliflower 102
Roasted Garlic Pork Supper 82
Roasted Lamb Rack 52
Roasted Pepper Sauce 46
Roasted Pepper Sauce, Spicy 113
Roasted Red Pepper Pizza .47
Roasted Tomato Sauce 114
Roll, Spinach And Cheese 46
Rolls, Chicken Mushroom 24

S

Salad
    Beef And Mandarin 11
    Crunchy Rice 96
    Pasta 97
    Potato 101
    Spinach And Pork 79
    Warm Pork 39
    Warm Potato 91
Salmon, Mustard Dill 75
Salmon, Mustard Honey 55
Salsa
    Fresh Corn 76
    Grilled Chicken And 76
    Tomato 68
Samosas, Chicken 146
Sandwich, Grilled Pork 78
Sauce
    Chicken 84
    Cool Yogurt 27
    Creamy Mushroom 116
    Ground Beef 86
    Lightened-Up Cheese 114
    Onion And Garlic Dipping 115
    Orange 66
    Parmesan Cheese 24
    Roasted Pepper 46

Roasted Tomato 114
    Spicy Roasted Pepper 113
    Sweet And Spicy 22
Seafood, see Fish & Seafood
Shake, Peanut Butter Banana 123
Shortcakes, Strawberry 120
Shrimp And Asparagus Stir-Fry 28
Skewers
    Ham And Melon 145
    Marinated Halibut 31
    Pepper Pork 38
    Pineapple Chicken 68
Slow Cooker Fajitas 62
Smoothie, Hawaiian 124
Smoothie, Piñana Milk 124
Smoothie, Strawberry Orange 127
Snapper, Blackened 27
Soup, Squash And Lentil 63
Spaghetti, Creamed Veggie 94
Spaghetti, Creamy Chicken 84
Spaghetti Squash Casserole 111
Spice Chicken, Poached 22
Spiced Potatoes, Crispy 100
Spicy Beef Pie 81
Spicy Roasted Pepper Sauce 113
Spinach And Cheese Roll 46
Spinach And Pork Salad 79
Spinach Mushroom Rice 93
Spinach, Creamy 106
Squash And Lentil Soup 63
Squash Casserole, Spaghetti 111
Squash, Maple Butternut .104
Steak
    Apple Curry Wraps 12
    Apricot Beef Casserole 58
    Beef And Asparagus 14
    Beef And Mandarin Salad .11
    Beef And Tomato Stew 57
    Lemon Garlic 16
    Slow Cooker Fajitas 62
Stew
    Basic Beef 80
    Beef And Tomato 57
    Beef In Red Wine 67
    Creamy Fish 29
    Garden Chicken 85

Stir-Fry
    Beef And Asparagus 14
    Oriental Citrus Chicken 21
    Pork And Pineapple 33
    Shrimp And Asparagus 28
    Warm Pork Salad 39
Stovetop
    Apple Curry Wraps 12
    Basic Beef Stew 80
    Beef and Rice Lettuce Wraps 77
    Blackened Snapper 27
    Bows And Fresh Vegetables 44
    Chicken And Pea Risotto 26
    Chicken Mushroom Rolls 24
    Creamy Chicken Spaghetti 84
    Creamy Fish Stew 29
    Garden Chicken Stew 85
    Lemon Asparagus Penne 45
    Parmesan Crumbed Fish 30
    Penne And Meat Sauce 86
    Poached Spice Chicken 22
Strawberry Orange Smoothie 127
Strawberry Shortcakes 120
Stroganoff, Chicken 51
Stuffed Zucchini 41
Succulent Lamb Chops 37
Sweet And Spicy Sauce 22
Sweet Potatoes, Mashed 103
Swirls, Pizza 140

T

Tea Biscuits, Buttermilk 120
Tenderloin (Pork)
    Maple Balsamic 34
    Pepper Pork Skewers 38
    Warm Pork Salad 39
Teriyaki Fish, Orange 74
Tomato Herb Pasta 95
Tomato Salsa 68
Tomato Sauce, Roasted 114
Tomato Stew, Beef And 57
Topping
    Apple 122
    Mashed Potato 87
    Tropical Yogurt 116
Tortillas, Cheese 147
Tropical Popsicles 136

Tropical Trifles 121
Tropical Yogurt Topping 116
Turkey Burgers, Chili 20
Turkey In Curry Sauce 49
Turkey Roast Supreme 60

V

Vegetable Lasagne 42
Vegetables, Oven-Fried 112
Vegetarian
    Bows And Fresh Vegetables 44
    Creamed Veggie Spaghetti 94
    Lemon Asparagus Penne 45
    Pasta and Cheese Supper 56
    Pesto Cheese Spirals 149
    Pizza Swirls 140
    Roasted Red Pepper Pizza 47
    Spaghetti Squash Casserole 111
    Spinach And Cheese Roll 46
    Squash And Lentil Soup 63
    Stuffed Zucchini 41
    Vegetable Lasagne 42

W

Warm Pork Salad 39
Warm Potato Salad 91
Wine, Beef in Red 67
Wraps
    Apple Curry 12
    Beef And Rice Lettuce 77
    Pesto Chicken 74
    Slow Cooker Fajitas 62

Y

Yogurt And Herb Dressing 101
Yogurt
    Cool Yogurt Sauce 27
    Corn Yogurt Dip 142
    Mashed Sweet Potatoes 103
    Pear And Yogurt Freeze, ...123
    Tropical Yogurt Topping 116

Z

Zesty Marinade 78
Zucchini Pepper Combo 105
Zucchini, Stuffed 41

Company's Coming cookbooks are available at **retail locations** throughout Canada!

See mail order form

Buy any 2 cookbooks—choose a 3rd FREE of equal or less value than the lowest price paid.   *Available in French

Original Series   CA$15.99 Canada   US$12.99 USA & International

CODE		CODE		CODE	
SQ	150 Delicious Squares*	CT	Cooking For Two*	CCBE	The Beef Book
CA	Casseroles*	BB	Breakfasts & Brunches*	ASI	Asian Cooking
MU	Muffins & More*	SC	Slow Cooker Recipes*	CB	The Cheese Book
SA	Salads*	ODM	One Dish Meals*	RC	The Rookie Cook
AP	Appetizers	ST	Starters*	RHR	Rush-Hour Recipes
SS	Soups & Sandwiches	SF	Stir-Fry*	SW	Sweet Cravings
CO	Cookies*	MAM	Make-Ahead Meals*	YRG	Year-Round Grilling
PA	Pasta*	PB	The Potato Book*	GG	Garden Greens
BA	Barbecues*	CCLFC	Low-Fat Cooking*	CHC	Chinese Cooking
PR	Preserves*	CCLFP	Low-Fat Pasta*	PK	The Pork Book
CH	Chicken, Etc.*	CFK	Cook For Kids	RL	Recipes For Leftovers
KC	Kids Cooking	SCH	Stews, Chilies & Chowders	EB	The Egg Book ◀**NEW**▶
		FD	Fondues		*May 1/04*

Greatest Hits Series

CODE	CA$12.99 Canada US$9.99 USA & International
ITAL	Italian
MEX	Mexican

Most Loved Recipe Collection

CODE	CA$23.99 Canada US$19.99 USA & International
MLA	Most Loved Appetizers
MLMC	Most Loved Main Courses ◀**NEW**▶
	April 1/04

Lifestyle Series

CODE	CA$17.99 Canada US$15.99 USA & International
GR	Grilling
DC	Diabetic Cooking

CODE	CA$19.99 Canada US$15.99 USA & International
HC	Heart-Friendly Cooking
DDI	Diabetic Dinners

Special Occasion Series

CODE	CA$20.99 Canada US$19.99 USA & International
GFK	Gifts from the Kitchen
CFS	Cooking for the Seasons

CODE	CA$22.99 Canada US$19.99 USA & International
WC	Weekend Cooking

CODE	CA$24.99 Canada US$19.99 USA & International
HFH	Home for the Holidays
DD	Decadent Desserts

Company's Coming COOKBOOKS®

companyscoming.com
visit our ↖ website

COMPANY'S COMING PUBLISHING LIMITED
2311 - 96 Street
Edmonton, Alberta T6N 1G3 Canada
Tel: (780) 450-6223 Fax: (780) 450-1857

Mail Order Form

See reverse for list of cookbooks

EXCLUSIVE MAIL ORDER OFFER

Buy 2 Get 1 FREE!
Buy any 2 cookbooks—choose a 3rd FREE
of equal or less value than the lowest price paid.

QUANTITY	CODE	TITLE	PRICE EACH	PRICE TOTAL
			$	$

DON'T FORGET to indicate your FREE book(s). (see exclusive mail order offer above) PLEASE PRINT

	TOTAL BOOKS (including FREE)

TOTAL BOOKS PURCHASED: $

	INTERNATIONAL		CANADA & USA	
Plus Shipping & Handling (PER DESTINATION)	$ 7.00	(one book)	$ 5.00	(1-3 books)
Additional Books (INCLUDING FREE BOOKS)	$	($2.00 each)	$	($1.00 each)
SUB-TOTAL	$		$	
Canadian residents add G.S.T.(7%)			$	
TOTAL AMOUNT ENCLOSED	$		$	

The Fine Print

- Orders outside Canada must be **PAID IN US FUNDS** by cheque or money order drawn on Canadian or US bank or by credit card.
- Make cheque or money order payable to: **COMPANY'S COMING PUBLISHING LIMITED.**
- Prices are expressed in Canadian dollars for Canada, US dollars for USA & International and are subject to change without prior notice.
- Orders are shipped surface mail. For courier rates, visit our website: **www.companyscoming.com** or contact us: **Tel: (780) 450-6223 Fax: (780) 450-1857.**
- Sorry, no C.O.D.

☐ MasterCard   ☐ VISA _____ Expiry date

Account # _____

Name of cardholder _____

Cardholder's signature _____

Shipping Address

Send the cookbooks listed above to:

Name: _____

Street: _____

City: _____ Prov./State: _____

Postal Code/Zip: _____ Country: _____

Tel: (_____) _____

E-mail address: _____

Gift Giving

- Let us help you with your gift giving!
- We will send cookbooks directly to the recipients of your choice if you give us their names and addresses.
- Please specify the titles you wish to send to each person.
- If you would like to include your personal note or card, we will be pleased to enclose it with your gift order.
- Company's Coming Cookbooks make excellent gifts: Birthdays, bridal showers, Mother's Day, Father's Day, graduation or any occasion... collect them all!

Canada's most
popular
cookbooks